THE
LATE
GREAT
UNITED STATES
CONSTITUTION

With Amendments
That Could Regain the
Liberty
America Has Lost

By

William F. Tofte

Acknowledgements

To the Founding Fathers, who created the greatest governmental document in history.

To my son, Joel, who first sparked my interest and love for the Constitution.

To my father, a true American entrepreneur, who taught me a love of country, the value of hard work, and philosophies of life that I will always cherish.

To my mother, who challenged me to seek truth and to pursue my dreams.

To the state and federal congressmen and senators who openly profess their love of the Constitution and who fearlessly raise its banner as the number one public issue of the day.

To my family, friends, and coworkers, whose deep concern for America's future encouraged me to write this book.

Preface

The United States Constitution is dead. Supreme Court justices, congresses, and presidents have so perverted its straightforward meaning, they have rendered it lifeless. The mere skeleton of democratic election structure is all that remains. The Law of the Land instituted a government that successfully brought about an America that has led the world in prosperity, freedom, peace, and goodwill, but has been left to deteriorate into rulership by a privileged elite. Government of the people, by the people, and for the people has been virtually nullified. The greatest government document in human history has been downgraded to near irrelevance.

The Framers established the Constitution with three basic principles in mind: self-governance, separation of powers, and limited government. Yet these principles, over the course of the years, have been forsaken. The constitutional power of the states and their people to self-govern is seen by many as a form of racism. Separation of powers is now regarded as unnecessary and obsolete. A limited federal government has been expanded to such an extent as to be unmanageable.

Some may object to the idea that the Constitution is really "dead," and perhaps other words could better describe its present state. However, if a person's heart has quit beating and their nervous system is shut down, *dead* is an appropriate word to describe their condition. Even after death, the hair and fingernails of a corpse continue to grow.

Many Americans are now realizing that the fundamental cause of all the major problems facing America today is the abandonment of the Constitution. We are learning that the

Constitution authorizes Congress to create laws only in specific areas and that all other laws are to be enacted by state and local governments. Against the constitutional mandate that it has the sole power of legislation, Congress has handed extensive regulatory power to unelected and unaccountable bureaucrats and agencies. We are also seeing that presidents have often acted outside of the scope of their constitutional powers and that Supreme Court justices and other federal courts are rewriting laws instead of ruling on them. We are discovering that all three branches of the federal government have so surpassed their constitutional roles that our government has outgrown its ability to manage itself, much less pay for its enormity. We are finding that instead of securing the blessings of liberty, this out-of-control government is threatening them.

There are millions of Americans, and probably hundreds of senators and representatives as well, who have not read our Constitution. Our nation's young people are not being taught its basic precepts. Many Americans have been led to believe that it is only to be read and understood by the legal scholar and the intellectual. It is not far-fetched to believe that some politicians do not want it to be read. If the general public were to become acquainted with the Constitution, we would quickly and conclusively see how politicians have politically and financially benefitted from abandoning it. To protect their closely guarded secret, they directly or indirectly proclaim the Constitution's irrelevance or illegitimacy.

Perhaps thousands of books have been written on the Constitution, most of them citing a multitude of Supreme Court opinions and historical events. Many of them, by an abundance of words, attempt to explain away its plain and obvious meaning. However, long discourses do nothing but blur the value and sense of its contents. *The Late Great US Constitution* is not intended to be a comprehensive examination of the Constitution, but to highlight some of its key elements and show how a governing elite has subverted them for political advantage in its quest for power.

The greater portion of this book has been purposely written without extensive referencing of Supreme Court rulings, scholarly dissertations, and "expert" opinion. After all, none of the framers were Constitutional experts; they created the first constitution in history. Does reading and understanding it require that we be? The Constitution the framers constructed explains itself in words they carefully selected for their simplicity, precision, and universality. When subjected to the renowned Kincaid test, it scores a 12.2 grade readability—the average high school graduate can well read and understand its contents. There is no need to go outside the bounds of the Constitution itself to comprehend, interpret, and apply it.

The Constitution is effectively dead, but there is hope for its revival and restoration. It is found in the Constitution itself—an Article V Convention of States. The Founding Fathers were well aware of the possibility that the federal government could seize power far beyond its constitutional limitations, and they gave the states the power to reign it in. This book includes several suggested amendments for the reader to consider as part of a Convention of States.

Table of Contents

The Great Constitution

The Late Constitution

Appendices   123

The Constitution of the United States   127

THE
GREAT
CONSTITUTION

Chapter 1
Words Are Important

*"The beginning of wisdom
is the definition of terms."*

—Socrates

Among all governmental and legal documents, the United States Constitution is the pinnacle of clarity, comprehensiveness, consistency, and impact. What its writers accomplished, many say, is nothing short of a miracle. Yet it is relatively simple and easy to comprehend. Understanding the basics of English and the meaning of a short list of terms, anyone can grasp its meaning. Only a few of its clauses are subject to debate, but even then, their correct interpretations can readily be attained by referring to the context in which they appear, other portions of the Constitution, or the Declaration of Independence. No constitutional lawyers or scholars are necessary. Our Founding Fathers worded the Constitution so that We the People and those who would hold office would be able to understand and apply its principles, mandates, and prohibitions. Equally important, they carefully selected its words to enable the people to easily recognize those who did not support and defend it.

In 1787, fifty-five delegates to the Constitutional Convention began the nearly one hundred days of deliberating, debating, contemplating, and recording the 4,543 words that would comprise the main body of the Constitution. If the average delegate spent only six hours per day at the Convention, more than seven man-hours *per word* were spent constructing the Constitution. (If the author had spent that amount of time writing this book, it would have taken him over fifty years to complete.) In addition, there were the thousands of man-hours spent in deliberation by members of state legislatures during its ratification.

Most certainly, it was the meaning of the words that was under such intense scrutiny. To withstand this extent of deliberation and debate, it was a necessity to select words with universal yet precise meanings. The writers carefully chose each and every noun, verb, adjective, adverb, article, and preposition. As a result, there is now no need for debate over the document's intent. The debate has already taken place. The Constitution means what it says and says what it means. Furthermore, it does not say what it does not clearly mean, and it does not mean what it does not clearly say.

Reflecting on some of the more critical terms in the Constitution reveals much about its character and purpose. The founding document, technically, is merely a group of words on a piece of paper, but the totality of its words and the relationships between them have the power and force of law. Below is a set of words that is critical in developing a sense of the tone and purpose of the Constitution and its Amendments.

Shall: Used 307 Times

The primary force of the word "*shall*" makes it undeniable that the Constitution is meant to represent the law. It is not a set of guidelines or suggestions. It is the supreme law of the United States. It is not a "living" document, subject to fluctuating interpretation. As it was written and amended, it is the final authority in questions of legality. The Constitution is neither liberal nor conservative, right nor left, capitalistic nor socialistic. It is above.

Democracy: **Used 0 Times**

Strictly speaking, our federal, state, and local governments are not democracies. In a pure democracy, the majority of the people living in a defined area are free to make all the rules of the government. Although they are different, democracy and anarchy are close cousins. The Founding Fathers were well aware of the dangers of a fully democratic society. While they understood that the deliberation of many could very well be beneficial in certain areas of life, they also foresaw the potential for mob rule. History is full of examples of such a danger.

Democracy is essentially a governmental structure that allows justice to be executed by a majority opinion without regard for individual rights. The Constitution, its Bill of Rights, and its other Amendments were established to secure those rights. The Fourteenth Amendment clearly confirms that the states must also operate in a manner that does not violate individual God-given freedoms. As stated in the Pledge of Allegiance, the United States is more properly referred to as a republic.

No, Not, Nor, Cannot, Notwithstanding, and Nothing: Used 105 Times

To secure the blessings of liberty, the Founding Fathers brought forth a set of laws—not to govern or restrict the people, but to limit the power of the government, particularly that of the federal government. The Constitution prescribes just what the federal and state governments can and, more importantly, cannot do. It is a predominantly negative document. Our elected representatives should be praised, not criticized, for restraining themselves from taking certain actions. Politicians at the federal level are often eager to seek the power to do things, but the Constitution demands that our representatives be leaders in restricting their own power. This principle of "no" is crystallized in the Tenth Amendment:

> *"The powers not delegated to the United States by the Constitution nor prohibited by it to the States, are reserved to the States respectively, or to the people."*

States and State: **Used 210 Times**

The Tenth Amendment, and other portions of the Constitution, divide governmental power between three distinct groups: the federal government, the states, and the people. The powers of the federal government are clearly enumerated in the Constitution, and although the many powers remaining are not distinctly named, they are nevertheless held in reserve for the states, counties, municipalities, and other levels of self-government.

In the Preamble, *the United States* is not so much a name as a description of the independent states that comprise the country. The capitalization of *United* and *States* is done in the style of the era. In today's writing protocol, it could appear as "We the people of the united states." The United States is a republic—a union of different governmental entities, the states, each with its own borders, cultures, elections, and laws.

This kind of union can be compared to the union of marriage. Two distinct and independent people are joined together as one. Each has their own personality and purpose, but they are legally and morally bound and in many respects act as a single individual. Yet, their individuality is not dissolved by the relationship. Likewise, the Constitution solidifies the preservation of individual states and their roles to govern according to their own constitutions through their own elected representatives.

Originally, the Constitution designated the Senate as the chief body of representation for the states. In 1913, by the rule of the Seventeenth Amendment, the election of senators by state legislatures was changed to an election by the people of the state. In passing this amendment, much harm was done to the principle of self-government and the separation of power as originally structured in the Constitution. The character and strength of a two-house Congress was dangerously dissolved. Once, the House represented the people and the Senate represented the state legislatures. Today, the two bodies are merely an amalgamation of representatives, one elected by a small group of people and the other by a larger group. The power of the states themselves has suffered as a result.

> ## *"We the People do ordain and establish this Constitution for the United States of America."*
>
> —Preamble to the Constitution

Many would be surprised to learn that the Constitution was written, not directly for the benefit of the people themselves, but for the benefit of the states. The colonists in the late 1700s already exercised their right of self-government through their state legislatures. With the ratification of the Constitution, the states authorized the necessary and proper power of a federal government over them all. The Constitution is abundantly clear about its intent to preserve the powers of state and local government against the powers of a federal government.

The force of the Constitution lies in its words. In passing a multitude of laws over the years, Congress has used millions upon millions of words, most of which they themselves have not read, much less debated. They fully expect American citizens to not only understand them, but to willingly obey them. All the while, Congress and its bureaucracies largely ignore the 4,543-word law that we call "the Constitution." Instead, they behave as a privileged class, eagerly making laws for the "lower class" to obey but absolving themselves of any obligation to submit the supreme law of the land.

Chapter 2
Government by the Governed

> *"We hold these truths to be self-evident,*
> *that all men are created Equal,*
> *that they are endowed by their Creator*
> *with certain unalienable Rights,*
> *that among these are*
> *Life, Liberty and the pursuit of Happiness,*
> *that to secure these rights,*
> *Governments are instituted among Men,*
> *deriving their just powers*
> *from the consent of the governed."*
>
> —The Declaration of Independence

For thousands of years and throughout the vast preponderance of human history, men, women, and children have lived under the rule of tribal leaders, religious clerics, kings, queens, emperors, and tyrants. Entire civilizations were subject to the dictates of leaders under whom they were born with little or no chance of self-determination. Their beliefs, thoughts, vocations, and social class were all established by rulers using various forms of governmental control—predominantly physical force. Independent thought and contrasting views of the spiritual or physical world were rarely tolerated, and at worst, were met with persecution or death. Yet the yearning for liberation from these oppressors and their institutions was not eradicated.

The spirit of freedom from the rule of the powerful was first documented in the Magna Carta in 1215. The seed of liberty that it established lay largely dormant until the 1600s, when religious intolerance and persecution, executed by the King of England, forced an exodus to the New World and the establishment of self-governing colonies. England's continued oppression and taxation of the colonies led to the documentation and acceptance of the principle on which a nation was founded—a nation that has led the world in prosperity, opportunity, and invention. The God-given right of self-government was recorded in the Declaration of Independence. It then led to the Articles of Confederation and ultimately to the Constitution of the United States. Our Constitution is the institutionalization of government by the consent of the governed.

The Constitution and the principles of liberty brought forth a nation whose accomplishments in the advancement of mankind are unparalleled in human history. The freedom of religion sought by the Pilgrims and other colonists ignited freedom of thought. Freedom of thought exploded into the high-speed advancement of technology. For the average man, woman, and child, that advancement has established a quality of life never before seen or even imagined.

In spite of its obvious and overwhelming success, government by the consent of the governed is still doubted, or even ridiculed, by some. Some religious leaders have proposed forms of government that they believe will be superior to it. Today, some highly religious individuals promote governmental establishment of morals-related legislation at the federal level, much of which seems dangerously close to simple religious preference. A growing group of religious extremists, here and abroad, reject the concept of self-government and will even kill those who refuse to submit to the laws they say *their* god has instituted.

The notion of governing by the consent of the governed is also rejected in the secular realm, regardless of the categorical failure of alternative forms of government. Communists, socialists, and tyrants all adhere to the philosophy that society is to be governed and controlled by an elite class of policymakers, namely themselves. Instead of governing by the consent of the governed, these political systems govern at the expense and peril of the governed.

Hostility toward the idea of governing by the consent of the governed is not exclusive to communists, socialists, and intolerant religious zealots. Opposition to self-government exists among some of our presidents, congressmen, and Supreme Court justices. The Constitution that We the People established is the documented representation of the concept of self-government. Therefore,

Any disregard or misapplication of its words by those elected or appointed amounts to a denouncement of the God-given right of self-government itself.

Chapter 3
Liberty Defined

"We the People . . . in Order to . . . secure the Blessings of Liberty to ourselves and our Posterity, do ordain and establish this Constitution."

—Preamble to the Constitution

"Give me Liberty or give me Death."

—Patrick Henry, 1775

The culminating purpose for which the Constitution was written was also one of the most famous declarations of the American Revolution—the passionate plea for liberty by Patrick Henry, a lawyer, planter, and governor of Virginia. The cry for liberty was shared by thousands of colonists who ultimately gave their lives to obtain it. But what is this liberty that was so fervently sought? Was it simply independence from England? We know that it relates somehow to freedom, but exactly how?

One can say with certainty that Henry and the colonists did not have liberty at the time, else they would not have demanded it be given to them. They clearly would not have preferred death to some vague notion of freedom. They knew exactly what liberty was, as did the framers of the Constitution.

Freedom is the absence of restraint. We are born with certain freedoms—God-given rights. Among them are the freedom to act, work, think, communicate, associate, and worship. No government can restrict these freedoms. Using law, propaganda, fear tactics, and indoctrination, government may attempt to deny inalienable rights, but they remain. Politically, total human freedom can only exist in a state of anarchy.

Some have attempted to define liberty as individual freedom to act in any way that does not harm others. Given this definition, one could rightfully drive at excessively high speeds and run stop signs and red lights as long as no one is injured and others' property is not damaged. While this definition may make some logical sense, it is not the essence of the liberty for which Patrick Henry would have died.

The Statue of Liberty, given to the United States in 1876 by the French, dramatically illustrates liberty. The French were convinced that the American Founders had created a nation like none in history. While Lady Liberty's torch and crown demonstrate that liberty is a light shining toward the people of the world, it is the tablet in her left arm that truly defines liberty. It is the book of law, headed by the Declaration of Independence. Notice that the tablet is carried in her left arm. This is emblematic of law created by her, not handed to her by kings or autocrats. Lady Liberty holds law created by the people themselves. Therefore,

**Liberty is freedom
restrained only
by self-imposed law.**

Many, mistakenly, have used the terms "liberty" and "freedom" interchangeably. Some claim that any law created that enhances our security diminishes our "liberty." It does not. Laws may restrain our "freedoms," but not our "liberty." Law established at the consent of the governed does not *diminish* Liberty, *it establishes it.*

Laws, from which justice is determined, are vital to restrict, restrain, or compel certain human activity. They are legitimate and just only if they are formed with the consent of those subject to them. Law creation by institutions or dictators outside the processes of legislation defined by the people in our Constitution is the antithesis of liberty. In the 1700s, the king of England and its unelected Parliament were governing the affairs of Virginia and the other colonies through taxes and a host of other prohibitions. Although Patrick Henry was subject to laws and taxes created by his own legislative representatives, he still saw himself as not possessing liberty. He and the Founding Fathers knew that the governed should be the source of *all* law to possess liberty. If they are not, they possess none of it. Any portion of law, large or small, not created directly by the people through their representatives is tyranny.

Governance by the federal government must also be by the consent of the governed. The Founders knew that to complete the full cycle of self-government, the people must establish the methods and means—that is, the laws—under which a federal government would operate. Thus, the Constitution was written and accepted at the Constitutional Convention, which began May 27, 1787, and finally ratified by the legislatures of all thirteen states on May 29, 1790.

**The *notion* of liberty
became
a *nation* of liberty
for the first time in human history.**

Chapter 4
Legitimacy of the Constitution

"Governments are instituted among Men, deriving their just powers from the consent of the governed."

—The Declaration of Independence

"We the People . . . do ordain and establish this Constitution."

—Preamble to the Constitution

The Constitution was ratified by elected representatives of the thirteen states in 1789. However, some might challenge its validity over two hundred years later. By what authority did the Founding Fathers establish a constitution that had no end? Is the ratification that took place still effective today? The answers to these questions are clearly indicated in the Declaration of Independence as well as in the Preamble to the Constitution.

A combined understanding of the first sentences of these two documents is all that is necessary to reach the conclusion that the Constitution is, and shall be, the legitimate law of the land. The basic subject and predicate of the Preamble form a complete thought: "We the People . . . do ordain and establish this Constitution for the United States of America." Merging this sentence with the sentence in the Declaration of Independence above, a single sentence can be created that, in and of itself, legitimizes the entirety of the Constitution:

"We the People, by the authority of the self-evident truth that governments are justly instituted by the consent of the governed, do ordain and establish this Constitution for the United States of America."

The force of the words is obvious. The Constitution was justly authorized because the powers that it instituted were established by the consent of the governed. Its contents are therefore legitimate and valid because We the People declared and agreed so. The Declaration of Independence proclaims our liberty in the self-evident truth that all men are created equal. The Constitution affirms its legitimacy by the self-evident truth of our right to self-government.

The spirit of self-government was first documented in the Magna Carta. Over time it matured despite hundreds of years of a less-than-successful mix of parliamentary rule and royal succession. By the time of the American Revolution, the concept of self-government as the only just form of government was forged into the soul of America. "No taxation without representation" typified the new citizens' belief system.

The constitutional proclamation that the people did "ordain and establish" this form of government further establishes its legitimacy. At first glance, using both of these terms could seem redundant. However, the Founding Fathers would never have permitted such a literary mistake. *Ordain* legitimizes the Constitution for the ages. In various religions, priests and ministers are ordained for life. Saints are ordained for eternity. Ordination carries the same weight purposed in Lincoln's phrase, "shall not perish from the earth." *Establish* set the wheels of the Constitution in motion. By using the terms *ordain* and *establish*, it was as if the Founding Fathers decreed the Constitution for the future, and for emphasis, just in case there may have been a misunderstanding, they also declared that the future begins now.

Including within the Constitution itself the means of amending it also validates its legitimacy. The Founding Fathers, confident in the comprehensiveness of the document they had created, nevertheless made reasonable provisions for its amendment. This was immediately evidenced by the first ten amendments—the Bill of Rights. Tyrants and egotists insist that power, once given, is unalterable. Wisdom and practicality say otherwise. A Constitution without a prescribed process for its amendment would directly contradict its idea of self-government.

To further punctuate the legitimacy, relevance, and power of the Constitution, its writers purposely used the well-placed identifying article "this." The phrase "this Constitution" is used not only in the Preamble, but eleven other times in the body of the document. With this simple word, they emphatically declare that there are and forever will be no other documents, precedents, ideas, laws, or edicts to replace it, either partially or in its entirety, and that their words clearly expressed and defined their intent. Therefore, those who wrote and ratified the Constitution were all originalists. Supreme Court justices who are not originalists defy the Constitution and disqualify themselves as supporting, defending, and interpreting it. The Constitution is the law of the land; it, and only it, and its legal amendments shall stand in perpetuity for the United States of America. Erroneous Supreme Court "precedent," congressional or state legislation, and presidential order cannot supersede, override, or change it.

At the heart of apathy toward the Constitution and of the direct and indirect attacks on it is the belief that it is somehow not legitimate. Self-proclaimed intellectuals often assert that the

Constitution is a "living document," subject to their own "modern" interpretations. Academics scoff at its "inadequacies" and claim it needs to be "transformed," ignoring that it contains an amendment process. Others argue that it was written too long ago and that the times and technologies are now so advanced that it is only mildly relevant.

Many elected to Congress and other offices pick and choose from its tenets rather than accept its authority to rule the entirety of their actions. They often sanctimoniously assert their allegiance to the Constitution and immediately follow their remarks with the popular political conjunction "but." Some defiantly believe their oath to obey it is merely a formality. Ironically, the rules defined by the Constitution that determine how representatives and senators are elected are seldom brought into question. Most of those elected hypocritically insist that election requirements must be observed in the strictest sense, at the same time embracing loose interpretations of portions of the Constitution that are not to their liking.

The words of the Constitution interpret themselves. Its declarations clearly validate its legitimacy, authority, relevance, and permanence.

Chapter 5
The Purposes of the Constitution

The Preamble to the Constitution concisely and poetically lists the six grand purposes the Founding Fathers envisioned for the newly established American republic. The purposes included two for the nation as a whole, two for the states, and two for the people:

- For the nation: "to form a more perfect Union, establish Justice"
- For the states: "insure domestic Tranquility, provide for the common defense"
- For the people: "promote the general Welfare, and secure the Blessings of Liberty to ourselves and our Posterity"

The purposes could also be viewed as being placed in chronological order:

- To correct the past: "form a more perfect Union"
- To stabilize the present: "establish justice, insure domestic Tranquility, provide for the common defense, promote the general Welfare"
- To solidify the future: "secure the Blessings of Liberty to ourselves and our Posterity"

A clear understanding of what the Constitution was intended to accomplish is vital to understanding the entire document. There are no other purposes of a legitimate American government than the ones that are stated here. Care must be taken not to diminish or broaden them.

"Form a more perfect Union"

The United States of America was established by the Declaration of Independence. The government of that republic was initially established by the Articles of Confederation. From 1776 to 1789, the forms of that government proved inadequate. Rebellions, strife, confusion, and instability were widespread among the states. The confederation was weak. A stronger union was necessary to ensure tranquility and alleviate the conditions that were threatening the welfare of Americans. The Constitution was to better define the necessary power and authority that would be exercised by the federal government and what would be provided by the states and the people, therefore forming a more perfect republic.

"Establish Justice"

The highest form of justice envisioned by the Founding Fathers was the establishment of the Constitution itself, including provisions for its ratification by the states. A nation's first act of justice is served when the powers it authorizes are instituted by the consent of the governed. Government imposed by military force or by any means other than the consent of the governed is the essence of injustice.

A system of justice is the foundation of good government. Where free people exist, there have and always will be those who wrong others. Failure to establish justice inevitably leads to the escalation of lawlessness and the decay of the freedom, tranquility, and well-being of the general public. Many nations, while they may have a voting citizenry that elects representatives and other government officials in a way that is similar to that of the United States, have not established adequate systems of justice. Their neglect to establish adequate justice systems allowed for the perpetuation and growth of corruption, crime, and violence, leaving citizens impoverished and in a constant state of fear.

It is interesting to note that this purpose contains only three words: "to establish Justice." The other purposes have a number of adjectives and other words to describe them. In explaining the purpose of "Justice," however, no additional words are necessary—in fact, their use would likely only diminish its overall scope and meaning. When life, liberty, or property is denied by the government without due process, or when these things are obtained by individuals or groups without contractual or consensual agreement, injustice exists. There is no such thing as a vague, indefinable "social justice."

In order to establish Justice:

1. **Government itself must be subject to law by the consent of the governed.** A fully ratified Constitution must be established.
2. **Laws must be made and the consequences of their violation must be defined.** At the foundation of governmental power is the power to make laws. The Constitution explicitly enumerates the various areas of power in which the federal government can legislate. It exclusively assigns this power and responsibility to Congress.
3. **Federal laws must be implemented and any violation of them must be prosecuted.** The Constitution assigns

leadership and execution of this process to the president and the Department of Justice.

4. **Fair and equitable processes for the election and appointment of federal officers must be determined.** The Constitution establishes justice for the people with the election of the members of the House of Representatives, for the states with the election of senators (later revised with the Sixteenth Amendment), and for both the states and the people with the election of the president.

5. **Final authority on justice and constitutionality must be established.** The Constitution assigns this responsibility to the Supreme Court.

6. **Federal legislative power must be limited.** Article I, Section 8 of the Constitution strictly enumerates the legislative powers of Congress. Laws that violate the God-given rights of the people are prohibited in the Bill of Rights. The power to execute justice in regard to specific acts of personal morality and acts of violence is not mentioned in the Constitution. This power and all other non-enumerated powers lie with the states and the people by the Tenth Amendment.

"Insure domestic Tranquillity"

No constitution or legislation can provide, ensure, or guarantee total tranquility to all individuals or groups. In response to the chaos under the Articles of Confederation, the Founding Fathers, no doubt, already had "states" in mind when they coined this purpose. This "domestic" tranquility was not that of particular households or individuals, but of harmony and peace "among the States." This phrase further emphasizes that the Constitution was established for the states. Had the Constitution not been established and ordained, economic battles or even military conflict between the states would have been likely.

The Constitution was successful in its purpose to ensure domestic tranquility, if only for the seventy years before the outbreak of the War between the States. However, as many of the Founding Fathers knew, the question of slavery still needed to be answered fully. The constitutional compromises regarding slavery and interstate commerce temporarily staved off the clash related to liberty, states' rights, and economic parity among the states. But domestic tranquility was gravely interrupted when the Civil War broke out in 1861. It was waged not merely over the moral issue of slavery, but over its detrimental effects on trade between the states. The war demonstrated that when individual freedom is harshly restricted, free markets are damaged. The Thirteenth Amendment, prohibiting slavery, brought an economic and civil tranquility to these United States that has lasted nearly 150 years.

While a focused reading of this portion of the Preamble is important to understanding it and the rest of the Constitution, it may also be valuable to note what "insure domestic Tranquility" does not mean. Is there any question that the Founding Fathers never purposed to ensure tranquility in nations outside our borders? Had there been any intent of the sort, surely the delegates to the Constitutional Convention would have included it in the Preamble. That it is somehow the goal and purpose of the United States government to distribute economic assistance all over the world is alien to the Constitution. It has been appropriately said that foreign aid, with its bureaucratic and diplomatic irregularities, is, in fact, taking wealth from the poor of this country and giving it to the wealthy of another.

Tranquility among the states is not established, but ensured. Obtaining insurance in the commercial world does not eliminate risk, damage, or disaster. It only transfers its cost. Tranquility, in this case, is not provided, but at the federal level, it is purposed indirectly by the execution of the powers enumerated in the Constitution. With the lack of understanding of the Constitution and the federal government's obsession with establishing bureaucracies in Washington, DC, today, it is surprising that a Department of Tranquility has yet to be established.

"Provide for the common defence"

The American Revolution was won by an amalgamation of state militias under the leadership of George Washington. Such a loosely connected military organization was not likely to successfully fend off any future foreign invasion or attack. The Articles of Confederation provided little in the way of consolidating the states' forces to provide a sensible means of military defense. A unified, systematic provision to defend the territory of the states was required at the federal level. *Common* depicts that unification. The Constitution provided various portions of this system. Congress was empowered to establish and regulate the country's military defense and to initiate military action by declaration of war. The president was named Commander in Chief when called upon by Congress to execute war or military engagement.

"Promote the general Welfare"

The well-being of the American people was foremost in the minds of the Founding Fathers. Their vision was to create a government that would promote economic, spiritual, and intellectual opportunity for every man, woman, and child. They realized that to do so would mean establishing features of a federal government that state and local governments could not effectively provide. The states, by their ratification of the Constitution, granted several powers to the federal government to accomplish this noble purpose. Among them were the following:

- Provide and regulate a military to protect the homeland
- Protect the intellectual and artistic property of artists, inventors, and writers by establishing national copyright laws
- Regulate and create a national currency and punishment for counterfeiters
- Establish immigration rules
- Provide a national postal service

Other means to promote the general welfare were to be provided by the states and the people according to the Tenth Amendment. This purpose is discussed in detail in chapter 13.

"Secure the Blessings of Liberty to ourselves and our Posterity"

This purpose, insomuch as it was placed lastly among the six, is the pinnacle of all the purposes. Securing liberty was in the minds of all the Founding Fathers as the paramount purpose for which the Constitution was written. Without it, the Constitution would be an empty shell of election rules and delegations of power that would neglect the fundamental spirit of America: liberty. Without a written Constitution, the declaration that "all men are created with certain unalienable rights" would be meaningless; there would be no legal basis to secure these rights. Although all persons have rights given to them by their Creator, history shows that governments, tyrants, and criminals are forever seeking to deprive us of our lives, liberty, and property. Liberty is secured through institutions of government by the consent of the governed.

The Constitution establishes five essential means to secure liberty and its blessings:

1. The structure of government to which the governed have consented—the Constitution itself
2. A system of justice and due process by which individuals who violate the Constitution are punished, property is returned, or rights are restored—"establish Justice"
3. Military defenses necessary to thwart or prohibit the efforts of foreign countries to deprive Americans of their rights to life, property, and self-government—"provide for the common defence"
4. Protection of citizens' God-given freedoms from both federal and state government overreach—the Bill of Rights
5. Allowance for the states and the people to establish self-government in capacities not enumerated to the federal government in the Constitution—the Tenth Amendment

Justice is a friend to both liberty and security. Liberty is not the condition by which all individuals are permitted to do exactly what they *want*, but the condition by which they have the freedom to do what they *ought*—as defined self-imposed law. Freedom of speech does not justify lying or defamation. The right to bear arms does not give us the freedom to use them indiscriminately. Freedom of religion does not include the right to participate in religious practices that harm others.

Law and liberty are not opposing forces, but brothers. Anarchy and lawlessness threaten both liberty and security, resulting in individual and societal misery. Some have said that some freedom must be sacrificed when security is gained, but the Constitution affirms that liberty is never to be sacrificed or left unsecured. The government cannot and should not attempt to protect us from any and all physical, emotional, and economic danger, harm, or calamity, but it is the solemn duty and responsibility of the government to protect our liberty. The Constitution does not balance freedom and security; it fuses them.

Chapter 6
God, Religion, and Morality

While the Constitution itself contains no references to God, the Creator is acknowledged in the Declaration of Independence. In addition, our pledge of allegiance, coins, paper money, and other official government documents acknowledge the existence of God. Many argue that such references establish a government religion and that this establishment is in direct opposition to the First Amendment. Such an argument is entirely without merit.

Belief in God is not a religion. God is a self-evident reality. The Founding Fathers plainly and logically agreed that since there is a universe, it must have been created. Atheists and others may argue that there is no Creator, but nature and existence itself prove that there is an Uncaused Cause, called the Creator, who created all men equal and with certain unalienable rights.

Religion is the practice of one's belief in God. It is exercised in certain religious ceremonies, rites, symbols, and words. Freedom of religion is the right of the people to believe and practice any theological ideology in any way they choose, but to do so in a way that does not hinder or endanger the life, liberty, and property of others. Whenever government goes beyond mere acknowledgement of God, it is arguably entering into a practice of religion and should be avoided.

Closely associated with the concept of God and religion is morality. The original Constitution of 1787 was silent on all questions of personal morality. Murder, rape, prostitution, theft burglary, and virtually all other crimes by individuals were never mentioned, and rightly so. As previously stated, the Constitution was written for the states as a means of controlling the behavior of the federal government, not the behavior of the people. States are allowed and expected to pass laws that attempt to minimize human vice and negative personal behavior in a manner acceptable to state and local voters that does not violate their God-given rights.

Over the years, there have been several attempts to use the Constitution to regulate morally repugnant behavior. The first was the enactment of the Eighteenth Amendment, or Prohibition. This attempt served only to create a powerful and murderous crime syndicate and to relegate a very normal behavior to speakeasies and basements. It was repealed by the Twenty-First Amendment. Also, while a noble and well-intentioned Civil Rights Act was passed in 1964 prohibiting individual and personal discrimination on the basis of race, color, and national origin, it has done little but create agencies of paper-pushing bureaucrats. Recent attempts to amend the Constitution or enact federal legislation in regard to marriage, abortion, and other personal behavior will most assuredly meet with similar results.

The need for justice and control of morality at the federal level is not so much a question of whether certain behavior should or should not be prohibited by laws or by the Constitution, but whether such laws can be enforced fairly, effectively, and practically from Washington, DC—they cannot. This reality is borne out by the abject failure of federal drug, hate crime, and other legislation in regard to personal morality. Such legislation is, and should be, reserved to the states and the people as mandated by the Constitution.

Chapter 7
Three Branches of Government

The purposes of the Constitution are a necessary foundation for the United States government, but they must be attained through the institutional powers granted by self-governing people. The fundamental institutions established in the Constitution are the legislative branch, the executive branch, and the judicial branch. The power to create laws, the power to manage and execute those laws, and the power to justly determine the violations of those laws complete the full circle of rightful self-government.

The Constitution establishes our government's operating structure in much the same way as a corporation establishes the methodologies and structure by which it conducts business. Missions, roles, power, authority, and rules must be determined for the corporation, its departments, and its employees (See Appendix 1).

Corporations and other organizations create mission statements and organization charts as a strategy to maximize their effectiveness. It has been said that it is not so much the quality of the strategy that produces results, but the execution of the strategy. Furthermore, organizations whose key employees do not perform within their prescribed roles in carrying out the strategy are doomed to failure.

Similarly, the Constitution is effectively a strategy by which to maximize human liberty and institutionalize self-government. By the Constitution, federal powers are held in check and balanced among the three branches, ensuring that, in the end, the essential power is retained by the people and the states. When Congress, presidents, and Supreme Court justices fail to carry out the strategy by ignoring their Constitutional roles, the country suffers.

Today, and all too often, Congress enacts legislation that is beyond its constitutional bounds, infringing on the legislative rights and powers of the people and the states. Presidents frequently refuse to execute the laws passed by Congress and instead create their own laws by executive order. The Supreme Court misapplies and misinterprets both the Constitution and congressional law, effectively *legislating*, and *amending* the Constitution from its *judicial* bench. The combined result is lawlessness at the highest level, and it is transforming America from a land of liberty into a land of tyranny. But the tyrant in this case is not a Hitler or a Stalin. It is now a three-headed monster called the federal government. The Constitution, as originally written, is dead.

THE
LATE
CONSTITUTION

Chapter 8
America Asleep

"The price of Liberty is eternal vigilance."

—Thomas Jefferson

From the signing of the Declaration of Independence in 1787 until the early 1900s, American history was punctuated with the unparalleled expansion of freedom, prosperity, and opportunity—the blessings secured by steadfast adherence to the Constitution. Through a tragic but unavoidable loss of life, the age-old institution of slavery was dissolved by the Civil War, the Emancipation Proclamation, and the Thirteenth Amendment. Women won their right to vote in 1920 with the Nineteenth Amendment. The blessings of Liberty were flourishing. In 1886, France donated the Statue of Liberty as a tribute to the hundredth year of our independence and the amazing results of self-governance and the Constitution.

Ironically, less than two years after the erection of the Statue of Liberty, Congress, for the first time, raised its hammer and quietly began to chisel away the forms of government that secured the blessings of liberty to ourselves and our posterity. With the approval of the president and the ultimate "blessing" of the Supreme Court, the Interstate Commerce Act of 1887 was passed, delegating regulatory power to the unelected bureaucrats of the Interstate Commerce Commission, in direct violation of the Constitution's mandate that Congress be the sole source of federal law. Effectively, a fourth branch of government was created, and representative self-government was set on a path of death by a thousand cuts. The Interstate Commerce Act of 1887 set an erroneous precedent that, over the last 125 years, has metastasized into the institution of hundreds of regulatory agencies and thousands of laws that bypass the required Constitutional legislative process. It was the first death blow dealt to the Constitution.

The year 1913 marked the creation of two institutions of power and the dissolution of another—the Sixteenth and Seventeenth Amendments were ratified and the Federal Reserve Act was passed. The combined effect of these three events marked a dramatic shift from the designed structure of the Constitution and left We the People holding a minimal position of power.

This phase of American history was followed by a subtly different one that began to take hold in the early 1950s. Congress began the era by ignoring its constitutional responsibility to declare war, allowing the president to initiate military action in Korea. This precedent began a seventy-year phase dominated by senseless war and loss of life.

As a society, our economic prosperity had lulled us into political complacency. Americans in great numbers began to assume that the governmental institutions would work as they always had and that their personal engagement in the political process was not necessary. While the public, for the most part, was asleep and disengaged, congressmen and presidents, as well as their lobbying interests in Washington, began to seize power and personal gain far beyond those of their predecessors.

In more recent years, America's sentiment toward its government has been changing dramatically. We see the light of America's beacon of liberty and opportunity rapidly dimming. We witness the younger generations being profoundly uninformed about the basic principles and facts of American political processes. We see increasing political corruption and carefully disguised abuses of power. We see the government growing beyond our ability to manage and control it. We see Congress spending money and accumulating debt with no regard for how to repay it. For the first time in our country's history, the majority of parents see a future for their children that is less bright than their own.

We see more and more political parties and candidates whose differences are not principled or substantive, but who strongly resemble opposing *teams*, battling to say and do the *right* things to get elected. Rather than focusing their political debate on the merits of the issues at hand, they resort to accusations and insults to get our attention. We want our political leaders to be statesmen, but they act more like cheerleaders and entertainers who resort to using catchy phrases and divisive political demagoguery.

We Americans love our country and feel a responsibility to participate in the election process, but we see too many candidates who are likely to continue down the old political roads to nowhere. We find ourselves in a spiraling whirlwind of chaotic debate about laws, regulations, rights, freedoms, problems, and solutions. We are confused and confounded. As a result, many of us have become profoundly skeptical, cynical, and at best, apathetic about America's future.

In spite of these obstacles, however, many Americans still cling to the hope that their votes and political activism actually count for something. They continue to search for an answer to the political chaos and threats to liberty and justice.

The answer to this political turmoil is our return to the largely abandoned Constitution.

The Constitution is the one political truth that shines a light on each and every issue of the day. It is the one set of principles and laws that elected officials of all political parties have sworn to uphold. It is the one document that should begin and end all political discussion. If it is common ground that is the prerequisite for any meaningful debate among our political parties, our Constitution is the abundantly clear starting point. Any meaningful political engagement must be grounded in Constitutional knowledge and principles.

In the following chapters, there are included several suggested amendments to the Constitution. It is not the intent of the author to have worded these amendments to the total satisfaction of legal and grammar experts. But, for the most part, they do represent changes that could correct and clarify some of the major Constitutional distortions of the past. In Chapter 19, "Constitutional Housekeeping," several amendments are suggested that serve the purpose of resolving, once and for all, questions that continue to cause political and social divide.

Chapter 9
Legislation and Regulation

—Article I, Section 1

Following the Preamble, a list of the purposes for which the Constitution was written, the convention delegates begin to define distinct and separate powers for Congress (Article I), the president (Article II), and the Supreme Court (Article III). Congress, consisting of the House of Representatives and the Senate, was designated as the body of the federal government to hold its greatest power—to legislate. The delegates created the process by which liberty, freedom restrained only by self-imposed law, would be institutionalized.

The congressional power to legislate is total, but limited and exclusive. The first word, *All*, indicates that there shall be no federal laws created outside of Congress itself. *Herein granted* limits any legislation to types expressly permitted in the Constitution. *Vested* makes it abundantly clear that Congress, and only Congress, shall establish federal law.

Constitutionally, therefore, Congress may not authorize the creation of law by another body. It may not transfer legislative power to any other entity for any reason or under any circumstance, either by legislation or declaration. Powers delegated to Congress by the people through the Constitution may not again be delegated. Neither the president, the Supreme Court, nor any other agency of the federal government is allowed to create law. Violation of this clear constitutional mandate is a sharp departure from the separation of powers so fervently established by the founders and a direct contradiction of government of, by, and for We the People.

But, in 1887, the slow death of this constitutional directive began. With the creation of the Interstate Commerce Commission, Congress began instituting what has now become a fourth branch of the federal government: the independent regulatory agencies. Congress began passing laws allowing federal agencies to regulate various industrial, commercial, and individual activities—it passed laws allowing federal agencies to pass laws.

Today there are at least sixty agencies that have been given the independent power not only to generate statutes, rules, and regulations, but also to adjudicate fines and punishments. By handing this power to federal agencies, Congress has, in effect, also given legislative power to the president, who has authority over the agencies. All this has been created outside of the constitutionally defined process of legislation through the House and the Senate, then signature by the president.

As "good" lawyers do, Congress and the Supreme Court have buried this egregious violation in cryptic legalese. The Supreme Court has ruled that the constitutional power to legislate is "plenary," that is, "all-encompassing" and therefore includes the power to delegate that power to other institutions.

If this is true, then Congress or its departments could also delegate legislative power to presidents, other agencies, corporations, industry representatives, or even political parties and special interest groups. Congress could delegate the power to regulate elections to the majority political party. Furthermore, if legislative powers are plenary, Would not powers of presidents and Supreme Courts also be plenary? Could not these entities also "delegate" their powers to other individuals or organizations? This Supreme Court ruling and others, have effectively voided representative self-government and allowed Congress to outsource nearly have of its Constitutional powers of legislation. (See Appendix 2)

Lawyers and members of Congress have arbitrarily chosen to define *legislation* and *regulation* as two separate terms. The definition of *regulation*, according to the legal dictionary of thefreedictionary.com,[1] is

> A rule of order having *force of law* [emphasis added], prescribed by a superior or competent authority, relating to the actions of those under the authority's control. Regulations are issued by various federal government departments and agencies to carry out the intent of legislation enacted by Congress.

To proclaim that a rule that has the force of law is regulation and not legislation is simply semantics turned upside down. Regulation is a type of law, and law must come from Congress legislatively. The Constitution itself clearly establishes that regulation is a power of Congress and that this power must be executed in the manner defined by the Constitution:

> Congress shall have Power . . . To make all Laws which shall be necessary and proper for carrying into Execution the foregoing Powers, and all other Powers vested by this Constitution in the Government of the United States, or in any Department or Officer thereof. (Article I, Section 8, Paragraph 18)

For example, the power to regulate interstate commerce cannot be executed through any other means than that specified in the

---

[1] https://legal-dictionary.thefreedictionary.com/regulation

Constitution—by the legislative process mandated. That is, the power to regulate must be exercised only through legislation debated and passed by the House of Representatives and the Senate, then subsequently signed, or allowed to become law, by the president.

Delegation of regulatory power has also been viewed as a "practical" matter. It has been considered an impossibility for members of Congress to formulate concise law regulating all environmental and commercial concerns that are "required" to protect consumers and the general public. (After all, representatives and senators need enough time to do important things like campaigning, raising money, and "conversing" with special interest groups!) No doubt Congress members enjoy the idea that they can vote for or against constitutionally created laws that gain them political favor with their constituents, but leave to the regulatory agencies the dirty work for which neither the agencies nor themselves are accountable. However, this is the fact of the matter:

The ends do not justify the means.

We the People established the means by which laws are to be created in our Constitution, and we expect lawmakers to adhere to that process. It is their solemnly sworn duty.

Yet Congress continues to allow this monolithic bureaucracy to lord it over Americans and their businesses with an unrelenting barrage of rules and regulations—all without our consent. This power given with no accountability has led to a tyranny of the worst kind. Rarely does a day go by in which an agency does not announce new regulations, hiring more and more agents to investigate and fine businesses and individuals who have committed "crimes," violations of rules of which they may be totally unaware. During calendar year 2016, Congress enacted 214 laws, but unelected and unaccountable agencies issued 3,853 rules—regulations with the force of law. Altogether, American individuals and businesses are now subject to over 80,000 regulations.

Regulatory agencies are a huge source of government waste and highly likely corruption. In November 2016, the House Committee on Oversight and Government Reform (COGR) issued a report titled *Restoring the Power of the Purse: Shining Light on Federal Agencies Billion Dollar Fines Collections*. Its findings exposed the enormity and gravity of the power delegated to regulatory agencies. The committee reported that from 2010 to 2015 agencies collected over $84 billion in fines and fees. The Weidenbaum Center at Washington University in St. Louis and the Regulatory Studies Center at George Washington University jointly estimated that agencies spent $63 billion in 2015 to administer and police the regulatory enterprise. At this rate, the cost to regulate exceeds the revenue from agency-assessed fines by a ratio of approximately 4.5 to 1.

Potential and, no doubt, actual corruption and misuse of funds collected from fees and fines generated by regulatory agencies are equally disturbing. Many of the agencies have been authorized to have their own accounts, apart from the Treasury, in which funds are deposited and from which payments are made. The COGR, in its 2016 report, also stated that "agencies were generally unable to provide detail regarding the **use** of such funds." Evidently, the power of appropriation given to Congress by the Constitution has also been delegated to regulatory agencies.

Not only are these regulations unconstitutional, but they are also expensive for both consumers and taxpayers. Each year, the Competitive Enterprise Institute compiles cost estimates related to regulation. It calls its report *Ten Thousand Commandments* and compiles costs of compliance by businesses (and therefore consumers) and federal costs of government administration. Results of the 2016 report alone are staggering and contemptible[2]:

- Based on federal government data, past reports, and contemporary studies, this report estimates regulatory compliance and economic impacts of federal intervention to be $1.9 trillion annually.

- If it were a country, federal regulation would be the ninth largest economy, ranking behind India and ahead of Russia.

- If one assumes that all costs of federal regulation and intervention flow all the way down to households, US households effectively "pay" $14,809 annually on average in a regulatory hidden tax. That amounts to 21 percent of the average income of $69,629 and 26.45 percent of the expenditure budget of $55,978. The "tax" exceeds every item in the budget except housing. More is "spent" on embedded regulation than on health care, food, transportation, entertainment, and apparel.

    As early as 1926, Calvin Coolidge warned us of the dangers of government centralization and bureaucracy.[3] "No plan of centralization has ever been adopted which did not result in bureaucracy, tyranny, inflexibility, reaction, and decline unless bureaucracy is constantly

---

resisted, it breaks down representative government and overwhelms democracy."

With dire consequences, Congress has willingly and illegally violated the Constitution and handed lawmaking power to unelected bureaucrats, desecrating the fundamental purpose of the Constitution—to establish

"Government by the consent of the governed."

A Suggested Amendment to the Constitution:

Section 1. *Any legislation, having been enacted by Congress for a period of not less than ten years, may be repealed by the President. Such legislation will become null and void one year after such a repeal unless overridden by a two-thirds vote of either the House of Representatives or the Senate.*

Section 2. *Any regulation legally issued by a body other than Congress shall become effective no less than 180 days after such issuance. Congress, at any time, may repeal such regulation by a two-thirds vote of either the House of Representatives or the Senate. The President, at any time, may repeal such regulation. Congress may override a Presidential repeal of the same by a two-thirds vote of either the House of Representatives or the Senate.*

Section 3. *Congress shall make provision for their timely response to Presidential repeal or regulatory act.*

one person owns the fruits of another person's labor. While slavery was abolished by the Thirteenth Amendment, it was partially reestablished by the Sixteenth. Income taxes create a system by which the government owns a portion of every citizen's earnings. Our economic freedom is dangerously compromised by the Sixteenth Amendment.

Although it is expressly allowed by the Constitution, the income tax system in its present form and under any reasonable scrutiny has proven to be ineffective, inefficient, and alarmingly subject to corruption, abuse, and evasion. The massive IRS code is a web of confusing and contradictory rules, regulations, forms, and loopholes. It has resulted in a multi-billion-dollar industry of attorneys, accountants, and consultants to assist companies and individuals in wading through its mind-boggling complexities. By it, individuals, corporations, and nonprofit organizations have been placed on the unsettling tightrope between legally avoiding taxes and being guilty of tax evasion. No doubt, the vast majority of taxpayers have unknowingly broken one or more income tax laws. In addition, lobbyists and special interest groups are contributing untold billions to members of Congress, who eagerly legislate new tax advantages for them in return. By it, the federal government, from its constitutional roots, has mutated into an institution of social and financial "engineering," deteriorating both civil and economic freedoms. Its tentacles have reached into every realm of American life, threatening domestic tranquility, the general welfare, and liberty itself.

How can the current income tax system, which provides nearly 80 percent of federal revenue, be revised or even replaced to answer these strong objections and yet provide the federal revenue needed? Proposed flat taxes and consumption (sales) taxes are said to be "regressive" and to unfairly tax the lower- and middle-income groups. The IRS Code, with its tiered tax rates, is hailed as being "progressive," requiring higher income groups to pay more of their *fair* share.

However, if one investigates the root source of tax revenue, both claims are clearly faulty. Obviously, in the current income tax system, as individuals, the wealthy pay more taxes directly to the federal government than the low- and middle-income groups do. Corporations that make profits pay a portion of those profits to the Treasury. This is undeniable. However, the fact to be determined is not who pays the taxes or how much they pay, but who pays *for* the taxes?

The following steps are involved in the payment of corporate income taxes:

1. Corporations purchase goods and services of other companies and pay the wages of their employees.
2. Corporations sell those goods and services to other companies or perhaps directly to the public.
3. From those sales and expenses, the corporations calculate their profit and pay the IRS a portion of it.
4. When consumers purchase the end products, they pay for the combined cost of all the goods and services.
5. And therefore, consumers pay for the profit made by all corporations involved in producing those products.

Who pays *for* corporate taxes? Consumers do!

The following steps are involved in the payment of individual income taxes:

1. Employees produce the goods and services of the companies for which they work.
2. Employers calculate individual employee pay and

deduct necessary payroll taxes.

3. Employers give employees checks for the amount of their pay, less the payroll taxes.
4. Employers send a check to the IRS for the combined total of all the payroll taxes deducted from employee pay.
5. Consumers buy goods and services produced by the employer at prices that include the wages and taxes of its employees.

Who pays *for* individual income taxes? Consumers do! Therefore, consumers, both directly and indirectly, pay for all taxes.

By necessity, the cost of all products and services includes the cost of the individual and corporate taxes that are paid. When the rich man buys a $50,000 automobile, he pays for a portion of individual income taxes of the janitor in the assembly plant. When the poor family buys $50 worth of groceries, they are paying for a portion of the taxes on the $1 million salary of the CEO of the grocery chain. Both pay for a portion of the corporate income tax expense of the company from which they purchased the automobile and the groceries. Because the wealthy spend more money on goods and services, they pay more taxes than the poor. Therefore, the present corporate and individual income tax structure is neither progressive nor regressive.

In the end, the current income tax system is smoke and mirrors. The progressive and regressive arguments are used as a political tool to gain favor and votes from the low- and middle-income majority. It creates the illusion that the tiered income tax system is fair because it taxes the rich more than the middle class and the middle class more than the poor. Nothing could be further from the truth.

The current income tax system should be replaced with a national sales tax. But since both can supply the revenue of the government, why change anything? The reasons for such a change are found in a short list of constitutional, moral, and practical principles. A national sales tax would achieve the following:

- More fully secure individual economic liberty. Since each act of consumption would require and include the payment of tax, purchasers would have the freedom to buy the products and services taxed, or not.
- Ensure the taxpayer's ability to pay. To buy products or services, consumers would necessarily have the means to pay for the products purchased plus the taxes on them.
- Be more cost effective to administer. It would be a much simpler system to manage than the immense regulatory complexities of the IRS.
- Be transparent and establish clear accountability. The entire adult population would know the tax rate they have to pay. It would be seen on every receipt, not hidden in the vast set of IRS schedules. If members of Congress vote to raise or lower taxes, all of them would be clearly accountable. Changes in the national sales tax rate would be on every front page and lead every news broadcast.
- End much of the lobbying, crony capitalism, and class animosity that raises prices and corrupts our elected officials.

Ratification of the Sixteenth Amendment to the Constitution opened the door for Congress to enact means to collect taxes based on income, the definition of which is forever elusive and changing. Up to that time, the preponderance of revenue was generated from excise, sales, or import taxes in various forms and was sufficient to meet the needs of the country. Most certainly, where there is an opportunity to raise more taxes and to do so with the unknowing approval of the majority, Congress will do so. Excessive federal spending is an easy concept to sell to the public since we are continually led to believe that *someone else* is paying the bill.

Members of Congress and other organizations who are leading an effort to repeal the Sixteenth Amendment and replace the current income tax system with a consumption-based tax system are the ones who are truly keeping their oath to uphold the Constitution and secure liberty for ourselves and our posterity.

A Suggested Amendment to the Constitution:

Effective January 1, five full calendar years from the year of ratification of this amendment, the Sixteenth Amendment shall be fully repealed. The income tax system shall be replaced with a national consumption tax system.

Americans for Fair Taxation[4] has estimated that a 15 percent national consumption tax would generate taxes of approximately $2 trillion. In 2015 collections of individual and corporate income taxes were approximately $1.88 trillion. Using these estimates and the following process, transition from an income tax system to a consumption system could be relatively simple:

---

[4] www.fairtax.org

- Leave the corporate and individual income tax code as is for five years.
- Decrease individual and corporate net income tax rates by 20 percent each year for five years (20 percent in Year One, 40 percent in Year Two . . . 100 percent in Year Five).
- Increase the national consumption tax by 3 percent each year for five years.

At the end of Year Five, individual and corporate income tax rates would be zero. The national consumption tax rate would be 15 percent.

Chapter 11
Money

Toward the promotion of the general welfare and the ensuring of domestic tranquility of the states, the federal government, according to the Constitution, needed to provide various features of government that could not be provided effectively by the individual states and its people. The federal government needed to have power and responsibility with respect to money, mediums of exchange. Under the Articles of Confederation, each state was creating its own money, which led to mass economic chaos among the states and between companies and individuals. The Constitution expressly denies monetary powers to the states and relegates to Congress all powers to create and control the supply of money. Article I, Section 8, of the Constitution defined those powers and responsibilities:

- Coining (creating) money and regulating its value
- Borrowing money for the needs of the federal government
- Controlling the use of federal money through the appropriations process
- Reporting to the public about the spending of federal money

Coins

Coins have been the principal form of money throughout history. Gold, silver, and other metal coins have been used as a medium of exchange between purchasers and buyers for centuries. Currently, in the United States, the Treasury purchases metals from mining companies at their market value, melts them, makes them into coins, and stamps their declared value on their faces. The declared legal value of a coin, more often than not, is less than the actual value of the metal from which the coin is made. This is why some, depending on the market price of copper, have illegally melted down pennies and sold the copper at a profit. Quarters were at one time 100 percent silver, but now they contain about 8 percent nickel and 92 percent copper.

Regardless of the market value of the metal, a penny plus a quarter still buys twenty-six cents worth of goods or services at the time of purchase. A silver quarter will buy the same amount of goods as a copper one. Why? Because the federal government, through the power granted to Congress in the Constitution, rightfully and necessarily regulates the value of coinage by stating that value on the coin itself. Without this constitutional power, the smallest of transactions could not be conducted without not only negotiating the value of the goods purchased, but also the value of the coins used in the exchange. If the value of coins was not regulated, transactions involving their use would bring chaos to a large segment of the economy.

Paper Money

At various times in history, paper money has been used by governments and financial institutions, including the United States, starting in 1862. With the ease and convenience of its portability, paper money has no doubt dramatically spurned economic growth. However, its use is not without problems, not to mention counterfeiting. Coins have some inherent value, insomuch as they are made of metals that have significant value in and of themselves. Printed money does not. It is merely paper. This fact represents a more difficult governmental dilemma. Because paper money is essentially valueless, it does not even remotely represent value itself. Therefore, like coins, the federal government must, with the force of law, declare that a twenty-dollar bill has that value, as stated on its face, "LEGAL TENDER FOR ALL DEBTS, PUBLIC AND PRIVATE."

Since paper money has no value in and of itself, what does it represent? The answer is debt. Today's twenty-dollar bill is headed by the words, "Federal Reserve note." The US Silver Certificate, printed before 1971, declares twenty dollars in silver to be "Payable to the bearer on demand." A note is debt, just like a car note or mortgage. Buying and selling using this paper note is essentially the same as one financial institution buying and selling packages of loans from and to another. Coins and paper money (notes) are simply mediums of exchange. Nothing is inherently wrong with either, but both must be regulated to bring economic stability to the billions of financial transactions that take place every day. The Constitution clearly and necessarily relegates this power to Congress.

Money Created by Banks

The federal government introduces money into the economy by printing or coining it. But there is a third way in which money gets into circulation. It is created by banks and other financial institutions. Individuals and companies deposit their money in banks, but the bank does not hold that money for them. It simply owes that amount of money to them. Banks, in turn, lend money, and therefore create it.

This process can be illustrated using Bank A and Company B. Bank A loans Company B $1 million for the construction of a new warehouse. Like the US Treasury, Bank A prints $1 million in checks (money) written to Company B to purchase the materials and labor to construct it. Bank A does not deduct that $1 million from its depositor's accounts, but simply accounts for the transaction as a debt. As a result, Bank A can produce notes (money) written to Companies B, C, and D, exceeding the combined deposits of its depositors.

These transactions create money that previously did not exist. However, it is vital to note that these bank loans represent wealth in the form of buildings, equipment, and other assets that did not previously exist. Economies grow and jobs are created through this necessary and valuable process. This is not a trick or gimmick, but has been a customary and legal practice of the financial industry for hundreds of years. It has helped create the standard of living enjoyed by Americans today.

Since according to the Constitution the federal government is granted the power of money creation, and banks necessarily contribute to that creation, banking activities can and must be regulated to some extent. The primary means of regulating banks in this regard is legislation of reserve requirements to which banks are held. Under current federal banking regulations, bank deposits can represent no less than 10 percent of the total monetary debt of a given financial institution. That is, a bank with customer deposits (debt to depositors) of $10 million can lend up to $90 million to others. This regulation, along with the creation of the Federal Deposit Insurance Corporation, establishes control over the creation of money and diminishes the overall risk to depositors should the bank fail.

Money Created by the Federal Reserve

With the Federal Reserve Act of 1913, a fourth process emerged in which money is created. Its effect on the economy is both massive and profound. This process, simply stated, includes these circumstances and activities:

1. The Treasury periodically needs to borrow money to pay the expenses of the federal government.
2. The Treasury, to meet this demand, borrows money from foreign nations, the general public, the Federal Reserve and other sources.
3. Its monetary reserves are often insufficient to meet the needs of the Treasury, so the Federal Reserve simply issues checks, or electronic transfers, to the Treasury. Currently, the Treasury "owes" nearly $2.5 trillion to the Federal Reserve.
4. The Federal Reserve "buys" securities from its charter banks.

By this process, money is created and introduced into the economy. It is similar to the creation of money through individual bank loans, but there is one enormous difference. Individual bank loans represent wealth in the form of buildings, equipment, and other assets. The Federal Reserve loans to the Treasury and charter banks represent absolutely nothing.

Some political figures have correctly described this as creating money "out of thin air." Others have described it as legalized counterfeiting. In an attempt to avoid public outcry (or even investigation), the Federal Reserve has endeavored to hide this process by creating a new economic term. They call it "quantitative easing," or "QE." It sounds sophisticated and complex, but the end result of the process is the same—money is created that has no value and does not represent wealth. Yet some may still ask: Does creating money out of thin air damage the economy? Not necessarily, but its effect can be summed up in one word: inflation.

When the supply of money is increased in excess of the wealth it represents, the value of money is decreased. In other words, when there is more money in circulation for purchases of the same goods and services, the price of those goods will increase. Inflation is not caused by the greedy corporation or entrepreneur, but by the Federal Reserve supplying Congress with valueless money to pay for the debt incurred by Congress's overspending.

In pure economic and business terms, government is waste. Since government produces no goods or services which are demanded by the open market, it creates no tangible value. It is like business overhead. Government is the overhead for the American economy. It is necessary for all levels of self-government, but it does not directly contribute to the production of goods and services, and therefore does not directly enhance economic growth. Federal Reserve loans to Washington do not create or represent wealth. They represent debt, waste, and inflation.

Since 1913, Congress has effectively outsourced a substantial portion, if not a majority, of its constitutionally granted economic powers to a central bank, now called the Federal Reserve. It is ironic to note that the face of your $20.00 Federal Reserve note bears the image of Andrew Jackson, president from 1829 to 1837, whose major goal was the dissolution of the central bank of the time, the Second Bank of the United States. Jackson abhorred the central bank and cited it as an unconstitutional financial monopoly that dangerously federalized financial power and was wrought with political favoritism. Under any reasonable scrutiny, today's Federal Reserve System shows more than a few telltale signs of being laden with the same Jacksonian concerns.

The following are some criticisms leveled at the Federal Reserve:

- It is a privately held corporation whose owners are unnamed and secret.
- It is no more federal than Federal Express, nor is there a monetary reserve held in its vaults. It is a financial cabal, an economic cartel whose purpose is to protect itself from financial competition.
- Its history is peppered with the names of the rich and powerful, including Warburg, Rockefeller, Morgan, Rothschild, and others, linking the Federal Reserve to the high possibility of crony capitalism and corruption.
- The legislation creating it was written by special interest international bankers and passed through Congress under highly questionable circumstances.
- It has monopolized the financial industry in the controlling hands of unelected, largely foreign financial interests.
- It controls hundreds of billions of US dollars in virtually unaudited books.
- It loans "no-cost," unearned money to the US Treasury, which repays the loans, principal, and interest on the backs of the real earnings of the American people.
- It borrows money from foreign nations under terms unknown to Congress or the people.
- It is not fully audited, and therefore unsubstantiated profits are said to be returned to the US Treasury, paying

its billionaire directors and owners first.

There is no question that the Federal Reserve Act, as well as the system it created, violates the letter and spirit of the Constitution. Mayer Rothschild, whose family was (and likely still is) a major player in the Federal Reserve saga, showed his disdain and lack of respect for any and all governmental authority when he said, "Give me control of a nation's money supply, and I care not who makes the laws." The Federal Reserve Act of 1913 has done just that. Enormous power over the supply of money, and therefore over the economy as a whole, was handed to a secret group of international bankers, where it still resides today. Economic powers relegated to Congress by the Constitution cannot be delegated to another institution, either public or private. These powers belong to Congress and no other.

There is no higher form of corruption than the possession and yielding of unconstitutional monetary power. It has been wisely said that the best way to end corruption in high places is to get rid of the high places. The Federal Reserve Act of 1913 should be repealed, returning control of the money supply to its rightful constitutional owner: Congress and the American people.

A Suggested Amendment to the Constitution:

No Congress, President, or Supreme Court, by legislation, order, or declaration, shall establish a central bank. This amendment, effective the date of its ratification, hereby repeals the Federal Reserve Act of 1913 and any related legislation. Congress shall have the power to regulate banking institutions and to create and borrow money, and shall not delegate this power, in whole or in part, to any agency, department, or entity, either publicly or privately owned.

Chapter 12
Spending

–Article I, Section 9, Paragraph 7

The Constitution lays out the legal process by which it creates money and raises revenue by taxation or borrowing, and by these two clauses, the process by which the dollars are spent. Any and all organizations control their spending through various authorization processes. The federal government is no different. The Constitution solely empowers Congress with the responsibility and power to control the expenditure of our tax dollars. The executive and judicial branches have no such control. Congress's failure to exercise spending restraint and control will inevitably lead to massive misappropriation of funds, governmental corruption, and inflation. Historically, financial collapse has been the downfall of all once-great nations.

The simple rule of not spending more than you receive in revenue is the universal model for economic stability. This rule has been successfully used by families and businesses for centuries, but for the last fifty or so years, its simple wisdom has been abandoned by Congress. Instead of wisdom and prudence,

Congress worships expediency and reelection by handing out pieces of the pie in excess of the pie itself.

The root cause of this obsessive spending and the resultant debt can be traced to negligence of one of our country's founding constitutional principles, "No taxation without representation." Future generations are paying for the overindulgence of past Congresses, for whom they never had the opportunity to vote. We are being taxed before being represented. It is the moral equivalent of theft—that is, taking money from someone without their consent.

To understand spending, several terms need to be clarified and their constitutional relevance, or lack of it, established.

- **Deficit:** The yearly funds spent by the government in excess of what it yearly receives in revenue.
- **Surplus:** The yearly revenue received by government in excess of what it spends yearly. The bad news is that only twelve surplus years have occurred since 1940. The good news us that surpluses do occur, but only occasionally.
- **Debt:** The accumulated total of all yearly deficit spending.

Instead of debt being the last resort in times of war or national calamity, borrowing has become the order of the day for Congress and the federal government. Recently, the national debt exceeded $22 trillion! The interest alone on the national debt for 2018 was over $500 billion!

For politicians to brag that they have reduced deficits is only to brag that they have increased the total federal debt by less than in previous years. This simply reduces the time it will take the country to fall over the edge of the financial cliff that certainly awaits. Unless our addiction to deficit spending is replaced with years of surpluses and elimination of the shameful national debt, the time bomb of economic collapse will soon explode.

Federal Spending as an Investment

To gain the approval of the public, politicians have also adopted a very businesslike term, *investment*. This is an attempt to promote the erroneous idea that government spending can actually stimulate economic growth. Be assured that it is simply another code word for spending. They theorize that putting federal money into education or research and other programs will produce positive economic effects. They roll the dice with our hard-earned dollars, knowing that the failure rate of such government spending is likely to be 100 percent. The fact is that since government produces nothing of real economic value, there can be no true return on investment.

The end result of all such "investment" is an increase in debt. There is no good or bad debt. It is all bad. The final result of deficit spending is inevitable quantitative easing, that is, printing money out of thin air and distributing it into the economy. Printing money stimulates the economy as much as printing high school degrees stimulates education.

Discretionary and Nondiscretionary Spending

There are no *types* of spending in the Constitution. There is only spending. We have been told by politicians that there is certain spending that must continue (nondiscretionary) and that all other spending could be reduced (discretionary). They delude us into thinking that there is some contractual agreement with employees to provide the published benefits of Social Security and Medicare. Who among us has signed such an agreement? Did we individually participate in "re-signing" a contract the many times when Congress raised the Social Security and Medicare tax rates and limits? How can the benefits (spending) be nondiscretionary, while the tax rates we are being charged are discretionary? These are terms used by Congress members to avoid the responsibility of the devastating economic calamity that will certainly come if we do not address the increasing debt, caused by overspending in all agencies of the federal government.

Debt Ceilings

Beginning in 1962, Congress has sought to restrain itself from spending and borrowing by establishing a debt ceiling. By 2015, it had raised the debt ceiling seventy-four times. It has been said that repeating the same process only to get the same results is insanity. Congress certainly fits that definition in this case. The political benefits of spending beyond our means have won over the practical and moral consequences of unsustainable increases in the national debt. Debt ceiling have not once restrained Congress from continuing to increase the total national debt. The Washington spending machine rolls on.

Budgets and Appropriations

There is no constitutional requirement that Congress or the president prepare a budget, but this legislative budget process has become a political tool used to convince the public that there is a rational and deliberative process by which federal spending is controlled. The Founding Fathers knew that, in the end, budgets mean nothing. Similar to the debt ceiling gimmick, they are merely plans, meant to be broken and changed.

The Constitution makes it very clear that the appropriations process, legislated by Congress, is the means by which spending is to be controlled. Each year, the choice to extend or end federal programs is in the hands of Congress. Where legislation proves ineffective in achieving certain ends (and it nearly always does), Congress can cut off funding for it. The appropriations process is where politics meets reality. Members of Congress seeking to reduce the national debt by cutting spending need to go no farther than here. Budgets, sequesters, and debt ceilings mean nothing at this point. Votes for the various appropriations bills that do not cut spending from previous years are votes for a continually mounting national debt.

If the need to cut spending is so obvious, why does Congress continue this practice of rubber-stamping last year's appropriations bills? And furthermore, why does our spending continue to increase? There are several reasons:

1. Around twelve appropriations bills come to a vote. Each of them contains hundreds, even thousands, of programs written into law thirty years ago or more. Going through them one by one to determine their benefit or necessity would be a strenuous process. Members of Congress simply do not want to work like the rest of us do. They would rather spend time raising money to get reelected.

2. On many occasions, to speed up the process, several bills are combined to make up massive "omnibus" appropriations bills. It seems Congress does not have the time to deal with the spending problem. It is easier to just kick the can down the road.

3. Most all members of Congress have their pet programs or agencies that they want to continue funding, insomuch as the benefactors of those programs donated heavily to their reelection. Voting to end funding for certain programs could cause party-to-party or member-to-member retaliation. Reducing appropriations and

defunding programs would rock the political boat.

4. Simply put, money talks. Members of Congress want to get reelected. They need donations from special interest groups to finance their campaigns. Special interest groups want the benefit (money) received for continuation of federally funded programs and will gladly compensate members of Congress for their votes to do so. Unfortunately, too many members of Congress are happy to accept those donations and vote for funding. The cycle of spending upon more spending is fueled primarily by political ambition.

If allowed to continue, current levels of spending and debt will have a certain calamitous economic result. With only a handful of senators and representatives who have the political will to vote to reduce spending, how can it be avoided? The Constitution has the answer. While Congress has the power of the purse, the president has veto power. Future presidents need to vow to veto any appropriations bills that do not significantly reduce federal spending, and force Congress to get to work on reducing appropriations from previous levels.

A Suggested Amendment to the Constitution:

Line item amendments and vetoes by the President are permissible for all portions of legislation which appropriate funds. Hereby, the President is only permitted to revise appropriated funds from zero to an amount less than the amount of funds stipulated in the portion of legislation received. As amended and signed by the President, such legislation shall have the full effect of law. Congress may reconsider such amendments by the President, and by appropriate legislation and a two thirds approval of either the House of Representatives or the Senate, the legislation shall become Law.

Chapter 13
General Welfare

The Founding Fathers envisioned that the establishment of the Constitution would promote the well-being of all Americans and they enumerated several federal powers to attain that vision. But sadly, phrases mentioning the promotion of the general welfare have been erroneously used to justify a flood of unconstitutional legislation. However, a simple analysis of the words of the Preamble itself destroys the flawed concept that the federal government can legislate any and all programs it deems are for the good of all people.

Note, first of all, the other verbs used in the Preamble:

- **Form** a more perfect union
- **Establish** justice
- **Insure** domestic tranquility
- **Provide** for the common defense
- **Secure** the blessings of liberty

All of them express finality, conclusiveness, and irrevocability. *Promote* seems out of place among these strong verbs. It does not describe a purpose that is a final condition, but one of progress and development. Businesses promote their products and hope for the best. Nonprofit organizations promote certain social values. The other purposes of the Constitution outlined in the Preamble are not subject to degrees of accomplishment. To promote a more perfect union, justice, tranquility, the common defense, or liberty would hardly be considered noble goals. Yet, *promote* is used here—why? The writers of the Constitution chose this word for at least two apparent reasons.

Practicality dictates that the government can never *provide* for the general welfare. It can only *promote* it—and there is a profound difference between the two. Providing for the general welfare is a financial impossibility. The welfare of the general public cannot be obtained directly, only indirectly. However, Constitutional *promotion* of the general welfare by the federal government is made possible by the following:

1. An effective and impartial justice system. The punishment and confinement of offenders diminish social lawlessness and create a more secure public environment.
2. A strong national defense, sufficient to deter or defeat any threatening enemy. Providing for this security is of critical importance to the welfare of the general public and to the economic landscape of businesses.
3. Other legislative and executive powers enumerated in the Constitution that could not effectively be administered by the state or local governments.

These three features of the Constitution advance the general welfare of all Americans by establishing an economic and social atmosphere in which individuals have a greater opportunity for personal achievement and success.

Promoting the general welfare by supporting defined groups or industries is self-contradictory. *General* means all-encompassing or broad. The opposite of *general* is *specific*. Legislation that monetarily supports specific people, groups, or industries is at the heart of corruption and crony capitalism. Congressmen seeking to "bring home the bacon" by voting for bills that fund particular interests in their districts or states are guilty of violating the constitutional mandate to promote only the general welfare.

The general welfare clause in the Constitution is frequently and erroneously cited to justify a now-incomprehensible list of federal programs. These laws *provide* specific industries with subsidies, tax breaks, and economic advantages. Legislation favoring or supporting specific individuals and businesses can never be construed as being for the general welfare and is therefore unconstitutional.

> *"The Congress shall have Power To lay and collect Taxes, Duties, Imposts and Excises, to pay the Debts and provide for the common Defence and general Welfare of the United States."*
>
> —Article I, Section 8, Paragraph 1

The above clause is the second of only two references in the Constitution to *general welfare*. This phrase, too, has been misapplied and misused to falsely empower Congress to enact any and all types of legislation. The clause is not about congressional legislative power at all, as it simply places the responsibility on Congress to pay for any and all legislation that it does enact. The Constitution and the Tenth Amendment remain clear in their limitation of powers to the ones enumerated in the Constitution.

Misguided use of the general welfare clause of the Constitution has developed into an all-too-common sentiment, even among Supreme Court justices. Their recent rulings effectively create laws that, in their opinion, are necessary to bring about positive social change. Congressmen and presidents also seem to believe that certain laws doing "good things" for certain groups is constitutionally permissible. It is not. To them, the unconstitutional bailouts of selected large financial institutions in 2008 were acceptable to avoid what they termed "certain economic catastrophe." The entanglement of the federal government in the medical industry was seen by some as a moral necessity. Educational mandates, federal student loans, food stamps, and other such programs are thought to be investments, contributing to some elusive social or economic benefit.

Politicians are all too anxious to *do* things for the good of their constituents, even though it means going beyond their constitutional power to do so. While they are driving America into disastrous debt and governmental overreach, they seem to be forever able to pat themselves on the back and receive the accolades of voters for all their good deeds. C. S. Eliot, an American philosopher, may have said it best:

"Of all tyrannies, a tyranny exercised for the good of its victims may be the most oppressive. It may be better to live under robber barons than under omnipotent moral busybodies. The robber baron's cruelty may sometimes sleep, his cupidity may at some point be satiated; but those who torment us for our own good will torment us without end, for they do so with the approval of their own conscience."

In essence, much of the federal bureaucracy could be put under one umbrella department called the Department of General Welfare, or more precisely, the Department of Doing Good Things for People. This would include the Departments of Health and Human Services, Education, Agriculture, Housing and Urban Development, and hundreds of other agencies. However, the general welfare clause itself, the Tenth Amendment, and the Constitution as a whole clearly forbid all of them.

The overregulation, red tape, high cost, and encroachment upon our individual liberties are the direct results of Congress members', presidents', and Supreme Court justices' misapplication of the general welfare clause. They are imposing their desire to do what they claim are "good things" for us over the limitations imposed on them by the Constitution. Again they are saying that the ends justify the means.

Chapter 14
Commerce

"Congress shall have Power . . . To regulate Commerce with foreign Nations, and among the several States, and with the Indian Tribes."
—Article I, Section 8, Paragraph 3

It was apparent to the Founding Fathers that the Articles of Confederation were insufficient to maintain healthy economic order among the states. States were effectively waging trade wars among themselves. Such conditions had to be resolved by adding provisions to the Constitution giving some controlling powers over commerce at the federal level. Was the intent of the writers of the Constitution to create a federal government that could regulate all forms of commerce and all types of goods and services, between any and all commercial entities? The constitutional answer is no.

Had the founders intended to regulate all commerce, they would have certainly stated so in the Constitution. They clearly did not. They specifically chose only three arenas of commerce in which the federal government would be involved:

- Commerce between and among the states
- Commerce with foreign nations
- Commerce with Indian tribes

As the diagram below illustrates, the three areas of commerce to be regulated by Congress do not constitute *all* commerce.

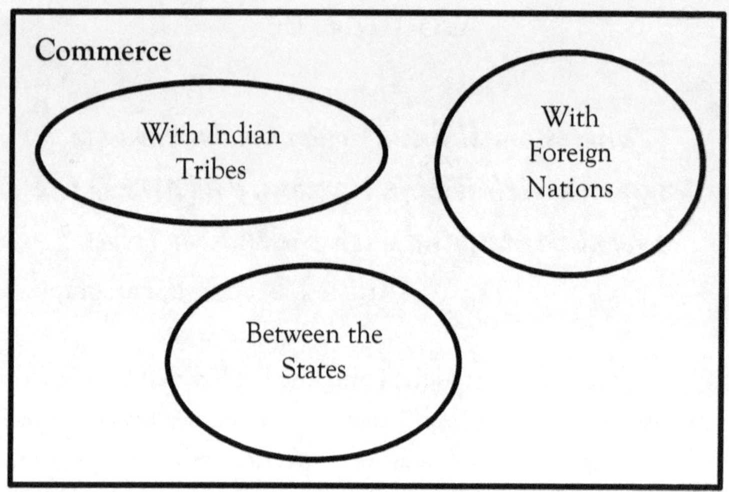

To further describe the limited nature of the commercial power given to Congress, the following is a list of some commercial transactions not among those listed in the Constitution:

- Commerce between individuals within a state
- Commerce between employers and individual employees
- Commerce between unions and employers
- Commerce between consumers and retailers
- Commerce between companies in the same state

The consistent theme of the Constitution was to limit the powers of the federal government. The case of the power to regulate commerce is no different. The states and the people, should they feel it necessary and proper, were to regulate all types of commercial dealings not specifically listed as regulated by the federal government. The Constitution contains no redundancies, ambiguities, or unnecessary phrases. Every word has a purpose. It clearly describes the limited scope of federal power with respect to commerce.

Supreme Court decisions allowing regulation of commercial transactions that "affect" interstate commerce have compounded Washington's predisposition to make more laws to "protect the public." The trouble with these rulings is that virtually all human events and financial transactions can be said to affect interstate commerce. Anything from birth to death, the weather to outer space, and lemonade stands to Super Bowls can be said to affect interstate commerce.

Unfortunately, what was intended to be a limited scope of regulation has mutated into massive federal control over any and all types of commercial transactions. Today, there are literally no commercial endeavors in which the heavy hand of the federal government is not involved. We now have the Departments of Labor, Transportation, Agriculture, Energy, and other unconstitutional bureaucracies that have created mountains of regulatory demands. More often than not, states, counties, and municipalities compound the regulatory burden by adding their own layers of bureaucratic nightmares for businesses and individuals.

Civil liberties regarding speech, religion, the press, and other areas of life characterize much of the political dialogue in America, but the idea of economic liberty is barely discussed. Does not the idea of liberty suggest that one has the right to manufacture, buy, and sell in any way possible, as long as others are not harmed or threatened? Strong systems of justice serve to prevent economic injustices from occurring. Overregulation of businesses is the equivalent of a police presence at the door of every household in an attempt to prevent crime.

Like all government, regulation comes at a high cost, not only the cost of regulation itself, but also the cost of compliance borne by the businesses regulated. Due to the high costs of compliance with federal mandates, American businesses are becoming less and less competitive in the world economy and are therefore losing market share and jobs to foreign suppliers.

Annually, the Heritage Foundation compiles data from hundreds of countries and establishes what it calls the Economic Freedom Index for each of them. This index attempts to numerically define a nation's economic climate and how easy it is for businesses to start and succeed. As of 2015, the United States ranked twelfth in the world. America, which established a Constitution that led the world in economic liberty, now ranks behind such economic powerhouses as Estonia and Mauritius (yes, these are real countries). This decline can be directly attributed to the federal government's overregulation of commerce and its failure to adhere to the limitations placed on it by the Constitution.

A Suggested Amendment to the Constitution

Congress shall not regulate the manufacture, sale, distribution, labor activities, and workplace conditions related to products or services conducted within a single state. No state shall prohibit the sale or purchase of legally produced goods, services, or financial instruments to or from parties in another state. Any and all legislation or regulation by Congress or states in violation of this Amendment is hereby null and void.

Chapter 15
War and the Military

"Congress shall have Power . . . To declare War."

—Article I, Section 8, Paragraph 8

*"The President shall be Commander in Chief . . .
when called into the actual Service
of the United States."*

—Article II, Section 2, Paragraph 1

The determination to go to war is the most critical choice any government can make. The human and financial sacrifices of war are beyond compare. Lives of soldiers and innocent men, women, and children will be lost. Financial resources will be severely drained. But war is often necessary. The wisdom of the Founding Fathers with respect to war is consistent with the principles of self-government.

Such a grave and consequential decision should be made by the people through their elected representatives. The Constitution places the sole power to initiate war in the hands of Congress. Its declaration is the first act of war in the same way the Declaration of Independence was our first act of independence. Military engagement led by the commander in chief is the second act. This power also implies a responsibility on the part of Congress for the country to engage in war, when necessary, or to refrain from war. No single person should hold this responsibility. Constitutionally, Congress and the people are to assume the risk and cost of failure or victory.

That Congress is to play the primary role in military defense as well as military action is clearly stated in the Constitution (Article I, Section 8). Beyond declaring war, Congress is given the power to raise armies, provide for a navy, establish military law, and call for military action to repel invasions and insurrection. The notion that since the president is the commander in chief, he has the authority to initiate military actions beyond our borders is entirely without merit. The Constitution clearly states that the president is to act as commander in chief only when called into the actual service of the United States. By whom and when is the president called? The Constitution again has the answer.

> *"Congress shall have Power . . . To provide for calling forth the Militia to execute the Laws of the Union, suppress Insurrections and repel Invasions."*
>
> –Article 1, Section 8, Paragraph 15

As is consistent with the entirety of the Constitution, the chief executive, the president, *executes* the will of Congress by commanding the armed services to actual engagement in military action. The president does not become commander in chief when inaugurated, but when Congress initiates military action. Congress first declares, then calls the president and the military into action. It is then, and only then, that the president becomes the commander in chief and directs the military action declared by Congress. There is no autonomous power of the president with regard to initiation of war. Furthermore, no treaty or United

Nations resolution supersedes our Constitution and the military powers it gives to Congress.

"Congress shall have the power to grant letters of Marque and Reprisal."

—Article I, Section 8, Paragraph 8

The power of this statement has been largely ignored in recent history, probably because of the unfamiliar terminology. Letters of Marque and Reprisal issued by Congress basically commissioned individuals or groups to capture and prosecute foreign criminals known to have committed offenses against American property or lives. In the end, Congress has the constitutional power to initiate any and all military or police action. The commander in chief is to exercise no such power unless called into service by a declaration of war or letter of Marque and Reprisal.

Unfortunately, since World War II, Congress has breached its constitutional responsibility by arbitrarily handing the power to initiate war and military style police action to the president. It has quietly sought to justify the abrogation of its duties in several ways. In 1973, Congress passed the War Powers Act, requiring the president to merely "inform" Congress of military action taken abroad. But can Congress legislatively allow the president to initiate acts of war in contradiction to its expressed constitutional responsibility and power to do so? The answer is a resounding no. Powers relegated to Congress by the Constitution cannot legally be delegated to the president without a duly ratified Amendment to the Constitution.

Congress's avoidance of its Constitutional responsibility to declare war has taken other forms. Congress has now been reduced to authorizing war. This is another attempt to avoid its constitutional responsibility. An authorization *allows* the president to act, or not act, as he or she sees fit. A declaration *demands* that the president act militarily. Authorization is a cowardly way for Congress to wash its hands of the dirty results of war, allowing its members to take political stances in opposition to the president's military strategies and method. If the president is successful, Congress members can still get some credit. If he fails, they can avoid responsibility.

Until 1950, when President Truman committed troops to the Korean War, there was no confusion in Congress as to its responsibility. Congress had declared war five times and the United States was victorious in all five. That is a war about every thirty years. Since then American troops have been involved in numerous military conflicts all over the world without a congressional declaration of war. Nearly 120,000 American soldiers were killed in Korea and Vietnam, and thousands more in Middle Eastern conflicts. Tragically, during this time, no clear surrenders or substantial victories have resulted from any of the conflicts in which the United States has been involved.

No war by the United States illustrates the dire consequences of our going to war without a declaration more clearly than the Vietnam War. From the early 1950s till the early 1970s, presidents and military officials both secretly and publicly engaged the United States in this brutal civil war. It all began with sending military "advisors." Eventually we were sending military equipment, then ultimately thousands of ground troops. The military "strategy" for winning included burning down villages, sending thousands of civilians out to fend for themselves, overtaking enemy strongholds only to give them up later, and devastating country sides and cities with more US bombs than were used in World Wars I and II combined. Military bungles, human atrocities, and war crimes were frequent. Nearly sixty thousand American soldiers died, along with at least two million Vietnamese civilians and military personnel.

Stateside, political unrest was widespread. Anti-war protests erupted. In the latter years, groups of anti-war Vietnam veterans joined in the demonstrations. Pro-war advocates paraded, not ready to admit that the Vietnam War was a huge mistake. Families were torn apart, not only by the loss of loved ones, but by political division. Americans were conflicted by their love of country and shame regarding the war through which they suffered. In 1975, the last American soldiers were airlifted out of Vietnam. Many American civilians derided American soldiers on their return. Few celebrated them. The anti-war protesters had called the Vietnam War "illegal," and they were correct. While American soldiers were true to their pledge to serve the commander in chief and to support and defend the Constitution, American politicians turned a collective blind eye and military leaders executed a war that the people, through Congress, did not constitutionally direct.

Furthermore, our soldiers are now being commanded to constantly engage in guerilla-type combat, leaving many of them mentally and emotionally impaired for life. As many as twenty-two veterans of Middle Eastern conflicts are committing suicide every day. Today, many Americans are justifiably "war weary." Peacetime seems to be a thing of the past. Near-constant war has become the new "normal." Since the inception of the undeclared Korean War, only about 56 percent of our days have been spent at peace. Prior to that war, it was about 94 percent (See Appendix 3).

No doubt the United States has developed military capability without comparison. Some have estimated that the nation currently spends more than twice the total spent by all other countries combined. Unfortunately, Congress has given presidents what seems to be a permanent pass to engage in war or military action at their sole discretion. It has been well said that if a man is given a big hammer, every problem becomes a nail. Far too many presidents since World War II have seen international problems as requiring an extensive military solution. The only true gains that have been made in recent wars and military engagement are the trillions of dollars in profit made by military contractors.

It is time that the American public rise up in protest and demand that our armed services be engaged in war or military police action only when our permission has been given, through Congress, by a declaration of war. This power must be returned to We the People through our representatives in Congress, as our Constitution clearly demands.

A Suggested Amendment to the Constitution:

No offensive military engagement or deployment, regardless of its size, shall be conducted by the Armed Services of the United States without prior written direction or declaration from Congress. Furthermore, without prior written directives of Congress, all military activities conducted beyond the territorial waters of the United States, including deployment, sales, training or grants of military goods and personnel to foreign nations for any purpose, are prohibited.

Chapter 16
Freedoms and Rights

About two years after the ratification of the Constitution, Delaware, on December 15, 1791, became the final state to ratify the first Ten Amendments to the Constitution, the Bill of Rights. Though objections were raised, few doubted their necessity and value. Other basic individual and collective freedoms and rights were at risk of being denied by an overreaching federal government. If these freedoms and rights had not been named specifically, danger of their denial would be well within the power of the federal and state governments themselves. Fortunately, the Supreme Court has largely kept the Bill of Rights intact, but attacks on it are both frequent and alarming.

Both politicians and citizens show considerable confusion as to the difference between freedoms, rights, and laws, but these can be explained simply:

- Freedoms are what God gives all humans.
- Rights are what government gives its citizens, for example, the right to vote and due process.
- Laws are what government takes away from its citizens; that is, it prohibits and punishes certain acts and requires payment of taxes, etc.

The Bill of Rights demands that freedoms of religion, speech, press, and assembly not be abridged, that is, that they be constitutionally protected and secured, and not legally circumvented. Government cannot give to citizens what is already possessed by them, but since governments throughout history have demonstrated the power to thwart, discourage, and even punish certain unalienable God-given freedoms, the Founding Fathers knew a Bill of Rights was necessary.

The list of individual freedoms and rights protected and given in the Bill of Rights is relatively short but comprehensive.

FREEDOMS Protected by the First Amendment

- Speech
- Religion
- Press
- Assembly
- Petition

Freedom of thought is the very fountain from which all our protected freedoms flow. Human thought, and its communication to others, has been the basis of human progress. Its value to positive social, governmental, and scientific innovation is self-evident.

Yet freedom of speech itself is now under attack from many sides. While grade-schoolers fully grasp that "sticks and stones may break my bones, but words will never hurt me," some college intellectuals are demanding "safe space," where use of phrases that make them "uncomfortable" is banned. Various institutions, including the federal government as well as powerful media corporations, have exerted power to thwart the broadcast of "harmful" political ideas and opinions, the very act of which impedes political and social advancement. But, to-date, thankfully, the Supreme Court has generally upheld law prohibiting the misuse of freedom of speech. Slander, lying under oath, fictitious accusation, falsely crying "fire" in a crowded theater, and other abuses of free speech are still illegal, and so-called "hate speech" remains a constitutional right.

RIGHTS Given by Amendments II–IX

- To possess reasonable means of Personal Security
- Due Process
- Trial by Jury
- Reasonable Punishment

Rights differ from freedoms insomuch as they are not God-given, but obtained from government. Free speech requires a brain and vocal cords. The right to bear arms requires a gun (or materials to make one), for example. Due process and trial by jury require courts and legal systems.

The right to bear arms and the right to due process. has also undergone attack. There is no question that murder with the use of handguns and automatic weapons has risen to almost epidemic proportions in the United States. Instances of mass killings, murder and terrorism are increasing at an astonishing rate. At the same time, innocent victims are being prosecuted for their use of firearms in their own self-defense, while perpetrators are allowed to go free. The right of due process is a right possessed by the accused, but it is also a right of victims and the general citizenry that all serious crimes be investigated and prosecuted by legal authorities.

Yet, any effort at denying citizens, much less punishing them, for use of a reasonable means of self-defense is altogether unconstitutional, impractical, and immoral. Furthermore, it is not unreasonable for the ordinary citizen to have the right to defend his or her life, property, or family with any type of weapon that is readily obtainable (legally or illegally) by the ordinary criminal or enraged mob, including automatic weapons.

Amendments one through nine, although threatened still remain alive, but not well. The Tenth Amendment is dead.

Chapter 17
The Tenth Amendment

"The powers not delegated to the United States by the Constitution, nor prohibited by it to the States, are reserved to the States respectively, or to the people."

The first nine amendments are strictly individual in nature. It is not until the Tenth Amendment that the rights of state governments are addressed. That states retain the right to legislate according to the needs of their own citizens was fundamental to the founders and critical to preserving government by the consent of the governed. Delegates to the Constitutional Convention realized that the preponderance of legislation governing human behavior should be allowed at the state level, and that a federal government should legislate and regulate only where absolutely necessary and practical. The Tenth Amendment punctuates a strict limitation to the powers of the federal government by reserving all other legislative power to the states and the people.

To establish "a more perfect Union," the Constitution needed to resolve the difficulties resulting from the Articles of Confederation. The delegates to the Constitutional Convention were abundantly aware of three distinct problems: one, that the powers of the federal government needed to be broadened; two, that those powers needed to be limited; and three, that state and federal law must never overlap or contradict. Federal law should never override state law. State law should never override federal law. Awareness of the dangers of these problems was at the forefront of the Tenth Amendment and all of Article 1, Section 8, which fully and clearly itemizes the realms of congressional legislative power.

The "necessary and proper" clause of Article I, Section 8, broadened and limited federal power simultaneously:

> *"Congress shall have Power . . . To make all Laws which shall be necessary and proper for carrying into Execution the foregoing Powers, and all other Powers vested by this Constitution in the Government of the United States, or in any Department or Officer thereof."*

Views that this clause enables Congress to enact any and all types of legislation in order to "establish Justice," "promote the general Welfare," and achieve what it sees as other "good" purposes, clearly violate the obvious meaning of the clause and the intent of the Constitution as a whole. Long, "scholarly" dissertations and multiple erroneous Supreme Court decisions cannot invalidate the Constitution's clear intent, by clear enumeration and declaration, to strictly limit the scope of the legislative power of Congress.

Over the years, Congress has passed thousands of bills legislating and regulating domains of American life that are not among those enumerated in Article I, Section 8, of the

Constitution, which therefore are reserved for the states and the people. Executing those laws requires an immense federal bureaucracy. The following is a "short" list of some of those agencies:

> Department of Education
> Department of Health and Human Services
> Department of Housing and Urban Development
> Department of Energy
> Environmental Protection Agency
> Small Business Administration
> Department of Agriculture
> Food and Drug Administration
> Department of Labor
> Consumer Protection Agency

Today, literally hundreds of federal agencies and sub-agencies have been established to administer a huge volume of federal law that are nowhere authorized by the Constitution. In the meantime, state governments are rightfully establishing their own laws regulating the domains of government constitutionally reserved for them. Few states, if any, do not have laws regulating agriculture, the environment, energy, education, and a variety of commercial and social affairs. As a result, American individuals and businesses are now compounded with both federal and state laws covering the same spheres and are doubly taxed for their administration and enforcement.

Regarding the Tenth Amendment, Thomas Jefferson may have said it best: "I consider the foundation of the Constitution as laid on this ground: That 'all powers not delegated to the United States, by the Constitution, nor prohibited by it to the States, are reserved to the States or to the people.' To take a single step beyond the boundaries thus specifically drawn around the powers of Congress is to take possession of a boundless field of power, no longer susceptible of any definition."[5]

The foundational clause of the Constitution is overwhelmingly ignored, undefended, and unsupported. Congress continues relentlessly passing laws entirely and clearly outside the scope of its power. Day and night, the Jefferson Memorial stands in full view of members of Congress, yet they turn deaf ears and eyes, willingly refusing to heed Jefferson's dire warning. Instead they support, defend, and even relish the powers they have ambushed and stolen from the states and their people. Their oath of office means nothing to them.

As though traveling the road to perdition, members of Congress continue on an unconstitutional path that is paved with their good intentions. Yet there are other subtle, but sinister, purposes. The more laws that are made, the more businesses and special interest groups there are. The more businesses and special interest groups, the more campaign contributions and likely more under-the-table monetary benefits. Is it any wonder Congress glories in what has become unlimited legislative power?

Jefferson's worst nightmare has come true. Step by step, Congress, with Supreme Court approval, has unconstitutionally availed itself of immeasurable, unmanageable, and undefinable legislative power, plunging the United States into spending, debt, and overreach that would defy even Thomas Jefferson's imagination. For all practical purposes, the Tenth Amendment and Article I, Section 8, to which it relates, are dead.

---

[5] From Paul L. Ford (ed.), The Writings of Thomas Jefferson, vol. 5 (New York: Putnam, 1904), 284–89.

Amendments to the Constitution are critically needed to revive and clarify the rights of states and to constitutionally legitimize federal law that the general public now views as necessary functions of the federal government.

A Suggested Amendment to the Constitution:

The rights and power of Congress and the States to legislate and regulate are hereby clarified by this Amendment:

Section 1. The powers reserved to the States (Amendment X) shall include, but are not limited to, legislation and/or regulation of intrastate commerce, labor, education, agriculture, health care, manufacturing, mining, and energy.

Section 2. Congressional power to regulate interstate commerce shall include (a) the power to regulate banking and the exchange of securities and (b) the power to regulate the manufacture, distribution, use, and disposal of substances harmful to the environment.

Section 3. Congress may enact legislation offering retirement and other benefit programs to individuals, but participation in such programs shall not be mandatory.

Section 4. No state shall prohibit the purchase of products or services originating in another state.

Chapter 18
Article V Convention of States

"The Congress, whenever two thirds of both Houses shall deem it necessary, shall propose Amendments to this Constitution, or, on the Application of the Legislatures of two thirds of the several States, shall call a Convention for proposing Amendments, which, in either Case, shall be valid to all Intents and Purposes, as Part of this Constitution, when ratified by the Legislatures of three fourths of the several States, or by Conventions in three fourths thereof, as the one or the other Mode of Ratification may be proposed by the Congress."

As it was written, the Constitution still stands as the greatest, most successful governmental document in history. However, as it has been interpreted by the Congresses, presidents, and Supreme Courts, the Constitution has failed in its purpose to sustain and secure the blessings of liberty and self-governance. When lawyers, thieves, murderers, and other criminals habitually find loopholes in the law, wise legislators attempt to close them by rewording or amending the laws they passed. To restore the Constitution to its original structure and intent, amendments are an absolute necessity.

In Article V, the Constitution provides two means of amendment:

1. Proposal of amendments by a two-thirds vote of Congress and their ratification by the legislatures of three-fourths of the states, and

2. A three-step process executed by the states without Congressional approval: (1) an application for convention by at least two-thirds of the states, or thirty-four states; (2) an actual convention in which states will propose amendments; and (3) ratification of the proposed amendments by the legislatures of three-fourths of the states, or thirty-eight states.

Wisely, the Founding Fathers foresaw the possibility that the federal government could subvert and expand its powers well beyond its constitutional limitations. They therefore included a remedy in the provision for constitutional amendment by the states, commonly called a Convention of States.

Although this provision has never been utilized, now is the time for such a Convention. Of its own accord, Congress will never restore legislative power it has unconstitutionally relinquished to presidents and bureaucrats unless its constitutional role is more succinctly defined by constitutional amendment. Presidents will not voluntarily return to Congress those powers ceded to them unless an amended Constitution clearly directs them to do so. Supreme Courts will repeat their return to their erroneous precedents unless those errors are clearly annunciated in amendments that close their imagined loopholes. Those powers must be restored to the only body that can constitutionally do so—the states.

Some fear that this approach would result in a "runaway" convention and ultimately reverse the principles of the current Constitution. Such fears are unjustifiable. Had that fear prevailed, the Constitutional Convention of 1789 would have never taken place and we would still be under the failed Articles of Confederation. Furthermore, although over the years, seventeen amendments have been added to the Bill of Rights, no such runaway conditions have come to pass. In reality, a runaway federal government began years ago. It is time for it to be brought back under the control that was established and ordained by We the People.

The movement to conduct an Article V Convention of States has already begun. At the time of this writing,

- COS resolutions have been filed in 48 states,
- 28 states have passed through one committee or more,
- 22 states have passed it on the floor of at least one chamber, and
- 15 states have passed COS resolutions through their legislatures,
- Over 4 million people support a COS.[6]

Thirty-four applications for a COS are required for a convention to actually take place.

It is time to trust the system of internal correction the Founding Fathers established in Article V. Left uncorrected, the structures the Constitution established will ultimately fall and the United States of America will crumble in the path of all great civilizations.

---

[6] Data provided by conventionofstates.com.

Chapter 19
Constitutional Housekeeping

American history is punctuated with various contentious issues that beg for constitutional clarity or correction. But for many reasons, these are swept under the rug or, like the proverbial can, continue to be kicked down the road. Several amendments at a Convention of States are herein suggested.

Racism

It has been claimed by many that a large number of both public and private institutions are wrought with "systemic" racism. As actor Morgan Freeman has suggested, one way to increase unity in the American melting pot is to simply quit talking about race. To facilitate this concept a Convention of States amendment could be instituted.

Suggested Amendment:

<u>Section 1.</u> No individual, nor private or public institution or organization, shall require, request, or record information as to the race or ethnic background of any individual for any purpose or reason. Furthermore, such records in existence at the time of this amendment shall be totally expunged within one year of its passage.

<u>Section 2.</u> No public or private institution or organization, in either a written or spoken manner, shall promote, in whole or in part, favor or disfavor toward persons of any race or ethnic background, nor shall they be or be named or self-identify, in

any manner, in a way that would indicate such favor or disfavor.

<u>Section 3.</u> Immigrants shall be required to provide statement and proof of national origin. Such shall be a matter of public record.

Public Display of Religious Symbols

For many years, many have argued that the display of religious symbols, phrases, and scenery on public property, by public and private parties, is a violation of the principle of "separation of church and state" and the "establishment of religion." In a Convention of States, this confusion can easily be laid to rest.

Suggested Amendment:

Display of religious symbols and phrases on public or private property by any person or institution shall not constitute the establishment of religion and shall not be prohibited by Congress or the States.

Federal Employment and Unions

Presidents from Franklin Roosevelt to Ronald Reagan have voiced the concern that unionization of Federal employees establishes an additional center of power, beyond the control or oversight of Congress or the President, and thus out of control of the people. Such power threatens the stability of the federal government and should be abolished.

Suggested Amendment:

The Federal government shall not employ members of an employee union or be subject to collective bargaining employment agreements. Within one year after the ratification of this amendment, Congress shall enact appropriate legislation to effect enforcement of this amendment.

Right to Life

The Founding Fathers never imagined that some in American society would consider that an unborn child is not a person under the full protection of the law. The most vulnerable of human lives should have the constitutional right to life.

Suggested Amendment:

The word "person" as used in the Fifth and Fourteenth Articles of Amendment to the Constitution of the United States applies to all human beings irrespective of age, health, function, or condition of dependency, including unborn offspring at every stage of their biological development.

Birthright Citizenship

Abuse of the Fourteenth Amendment by foreign nationals to obtain United States citizenship for their children is rampant. By this abuse, children of legal foreign visitors and illegal aliens have acquired full citizenship. This abuse must be stopped.

Suggested Amendment:

Citizenship shall be awarded all persons born in the United States of parents, one of whom is: (1) a US citizen or national, (2) a lawful permanent resident alien whose residence is in the United States, or (3) an alien performing active service in the US Armed Forces.

Term Limits for Congress

States, Counties, and municipalities have long mandated term limits as a way to curb corruption and limit public office holders from becoming professional politicians.   U.S. Congressmen and women will NEVER institute term limits for themselves.   Term limits for Congress must be enstated by amendment at a Convention of States.

Suggested Amendment:

<u>Section 1.</u> No person who has served four terms as a representative shall be eligible for election to the House of Representatives. For the purposes of this section, the election of a person to fill a vacancy in the House of Representatives shall be included as one term in determining the number of terms that such person has served as a Representative if the person fills the vacancy for more than one year.

<u>Section 2.</u> No person who has served two terms as a senator shall be eligible for election or appointment to the Senate. For the purposes of this section, the election or appointment of a person to fill a vacancy in the Senate shall be included as one term in determining the number of terms that such person has served as a senator if the person fills the vacancy for more than three years.

Section 3. *No term beginning before the date of ratification of this article shall be taken into account in determining eligibility for election or appointment under this article.*

Impeachment

Four times in American history, the House of Representatives have initiated proceedings toward the impeachment of a President. In no case, was the President removed from office. One President resigned in advance of his anticipated removal. The result of these efforts was only political chaos, division, and a waste of time and money. A mere majority vote by the House of Representatives to initiate impeachment proceedings is insufficient to prevent the political theater that inevitably ensues.

Suggested Amendment:

Any and all impeachment proceedings against a President, Vice President, or any other office holder shall ensue only by a two-thirds vote of the House of Representatives. Furthermore, articles of impeachment for high crimes and misdemeanors by the House of Representatives must cite violations of specific Congressionally legislated law and shall be delivered to the Senate within seven days of their approval by the House of Representatives. Otherwise, any such impeachment orders are null and void and shall not be considered by the Senate.

Emergencies

The Constitution, as written and amended to date, is silent in establishing institutional processes to deal with emergencies. As a result, both Presidents, Governors, and local authorities, have taken actions that are arbitrary and often capricious and politically motivated. The Covid19 pandemic has brought this issued to the forefront, as governors and mayors have been forced to take drastic, UNLEGISLATED action attempting to curb, slow, or eradicate the disease. Such actions may be well- intended and necessary, but nevertheless should be subject to the approval of the people through their representatives. The principle of self-government must prevail, even under the most unpredictable of circumstances.

Suggested Amendment:

Governors of each State may declare a state of emergency at their discretion. Each such declaration shall define (1) if not to the entire state, the jurisdiction(s) or the precise geographic area to which it applies, (2) a general description of the actions of the state to be taken, and (3) whether compliance to its terms is mandatory or voluntary. Terms of any such declaration shall apply for a period not to exceed fourteen days. Furthermore, State Legislatures shall make provision for their timely response to emergency declarations and may revoke or amend each such declaration, and its terms at any time. Mandatory compliance to emergency declarations by Congress, the President and all other governmental entities within a state is prohibited.

The Supreme Court

Usually for political reasons, Congress occasionally makes an effort to change the number of Supreme Court Justices. Its commonly called, "stacking" the court. This needs to stop.

Suggested Amendment:

The Supreme Court shall have nine, and only nine, Justices.

Chapter 20
Keeping the Republic

*"When Injustice becomes Law,
Resistance becomes Duty."*

—Thomas Jefferson

The story is told that soon after the completion of the writing of the Constitution, Benjamin Franklin was approached by a woman with a question. "Mr. Franklin," she asked, "do we have a monarchy or a republic?" The wise Franklin replied, "A republic, madam, if you can keep it."

Benjamin Franklin's reply expressed the sobering reality that our constitutional republic would be under a continual threat of loss. He also wisely understood that it is the duty of the American people to see that it is preserved. He saw that if the American public did not vigilantly protect the fundamental principles of the Constitution upon which the republic was built, the power of We the People would be handed to self-serving institutions, both public and private.

Franklin knew that such a transfer of power, if allowed to grow, would gradually but ultimately lead to economic servitude, suppression, and tyranny. In the modern era, Dwight D. Eisenhower, president from 1954 to 1961 and a World War II general, stated a similar thought during his final days in office, when he warned us of this now imminent threat: "Beware of the military-industrial complex."

The Pledge of Allegiance begs our resistance to the slow and steady deterioration of the separation of powers established in the Constitution:

"I pledge allegiance to the flag of the United States of America,
And to the Republic for which it stands.
One nation, under God, indivisible, with Liberty and Justice for All."

The American flag to which we pledge our allegiance is a symbol of the republic. That republic was built on the foundation of the Constitution. The highest form of justice is the one that establishes government by the consent of the governed, as is their self-evident and God-given right. Deviation from a government so established is therefore the highest form of injustice. It is *the* injustice that it is our duty to resist. If the country we love is to be preserved, there must be a return to the Constitution that established it.

We the People must fight to preserve and restore the Constitution. By amendment, election, proclamation, and demonstration, we must reject those who have violated their sacred oath to obey it. It is not only a shield of justice and liberty, but a light we must shine into the eyes, minds, and hearts of all who have not learned of its legitimacy and power. It is the Constitution that must be thrust to the forefront of all political discourse. It is the beacon of Liberty to ourselves and the world. Restoration of its original principles is the foundational issue of all American issues.

Appendix 1
Corporate and Constitutional Structure

CORPORATIONS	THE CONSTITUTION
Stockholders own the corporation.	The people and the states constitute the basis of governmental power.
The bylaws by which the corporation operates are established.	The Constitution is ratified by the states.
A written corporate vision or mission is established.	The Constitution declares its purposes in the Preamble.
The Board of Directors names the officers of the corporation and establishes their roles, authority, and responsibilities.	The Constitution establishes the powers, roles, and responsibilities of the legislative branch (Congress), the executive branch (the president), and the judicial branch (the Supreme Court).
Stockholders elect the Board of Directors.	The House of Representatives is elected by the people of each district in the states; senators were elected originally by state legislatures, now by the people of the states; the president and vice president are elected by the people through the Electoral College process; Supreme Court justices are nominated by the president and confirmed by Congress.
The Board of Directors, or the officers they appoint, establish the rules and procedures under which the corporation and its employees operate.	Rules and procedures by which the government operates, and under which the people are expected to live without compromising their liberties, are established by the Constitution and congressional legislation.

Appendix 2
Article 1, Section 8

Powers unconstitutionally delegated, in whole or in part, to the bureaucratic state or the president are noted in bold type and underlined below:

The Congress shall have Power To lay and collect Taxes, Duties, Imposts and Excises, to pay the Debts and provide for the common Defence and general Welfare of the United States; but all Duties, Imposts and Excises shall be uniform throughout the United States;

<u>To borrow Money on the credit of the United States;</u>

<u>To regulate Commerce with foreign Nations, and among the several States, and with the Indian Tribes;</u>

To establish an uniform Rule of Naturalization, and uniform Laws on the subject of Bankruptcies throughout the United States;

<u>To coin Money, regulate the Value thereof</u>, and of foreign Coin, and fix the Standard of Weights and Measures;

To provide for the Punishment of counterfeiting the Securities and current Coin of the United States;

To establish Post Offices and post Roads;

To promote the Progress of Science and useful Arts, by securing for limited Times to Authors and Inventors the exclusive Right to their respective Writings and Discoveries;

To constitute Tribunals inferior to the supreme Court;

To define and punish Piracies and Felonies committed on the high Seas, and Offences against the Law of Nations;

<u>To declare War, grant Letters of Marque and Reprisal, and make Rules concerning Captures on Land and Water;</u>

<u>To raise and support Armies, but no Appropriation of Money to that Use shall be for a longer Term than two Years;</u>

<u>To provide and maintain a Navy;</u>

<u>To make Rules for the Government and Regulation of the land and naval Forces;</u>

<u>To provide for calling forth the Militia to execute the Laws of the Union, suppress Insurrections and repel Invasions;</u>

To provide for organizing, arming, and disciplining, the Militia, and for governing such Part of them as may be employed in the Service of the United States, reserving to the States respectively, the Appointment of the Officers, and the Authority of training the Militia according to the discipline prescribed by Congress;

To exercise exclusive Legislation in all Cases whatsoever, over such District (not exceeding ten Miles square) as may, by Cession of particular States, and the Acceptance of Congress, become the Seat of the Government of the United States, and to exercise like Authority over all Places purchased by the Consent of the Legislature of the State in which the Same shall be, for the Erection of Forts, Magazines, Arsenals, dock-Yards, and other needful Buildings;—And

To make all Laws which shall be necessary and proper for carrying into Execution the foregoing Powers, and all other Powers vested by this Constitution in the Government of the United States, or in any Department or Officer thereof.

Appendix 3

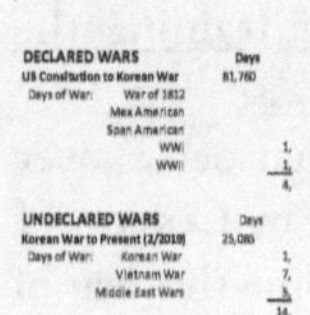

War Days % During Periods of Declared Wars Vs Undeclared Wars

DECLARED WARS				War Days %
	Date Begun	Date Ended	Days	
USConstution to Korean War	5/29/1790	6/25/1950	**81,760**	
War of 1812	6/18/1812	12/24/1814	919	
Mex American	5/13/1846	2/2/1848	630	
Span American	6/18/1898	12/10/1898	175	
WWI	4/6/1917	9/29/1921	1,637	
WWII	12/8/1941	9/2/1945	1,364	
			4,725	**5.8%**
UNDECLARED WARS				
Korean War to Present	6/25/1950	2/28/2019	**25,085**	
Korean War	6/25/1950	7/27/1953	1,128	
Vietnam War	11/1/1955	4/30/1975	7,120	
Middle East Wars	3/19/2003	2/28/2019	5,825	
			14,073	**56.1%**

The United States Constitution

We the People of the United States, in Order to form a more perfect Union, establish Justice, insure domestic Tranquility, provide for the common defence, promote the general Welfare, and secure the Blessings of Liberty to ourselves and our Posterity, do ordain and establish this Constitution for the United States of America.

Article I.

Section 1.

All legislative Powers herein granted shall be vested in a Congress of the United States, which shall consist of a Senate and House of Representatives.

Section 2.

The House of Representatives shall be composed of Members chosen every second Year by the People of the several States, and the Electors in each State shall have the Qualifications requisite for Electors of the most numerous Branch of the State Legislature.

No Person shall be a Representative who shall not have attained to the Age of twenty five Years, and been seven Years a Citizen of the United States, and who shall not, when elected, be an Inhabitant of that State in which he shall be chosen.

Representatives and direct Taxes shall be apportioned among the several States which may be included within this Union, according to their respective Numbers, which shall be determined by adding to the whole Number of free Persons, including those bound to Service for a Term of Years, and excluding Indians not taxed, three fifths of all other Persons. The actual Enumeration shall be made within three Years after the first Meeting of the Congress of the United States, and within every subsequent Term of ten Years, in such Manner as they shall by Law direct. The Number of Representatives shall not exceed one for every thirty Thousand, but each State shall have at Least one Representative; and until such enumeration shall be made, the State of New Hampshire shall be entitled to chuse three, Massachusetts eight,

Rhode-Island and Providence Plantations one, Connecticut five, New-York six, New Jersey four, Pennsylvania eight, Delaware one, Maryland six, Virginia ten, North Carolina five, South Carolina five, and Georgia three.

When vacancies happen in the Representation from any State, the Executive Authority thereof shall issue Writs of Election to fill such Vacancies.

The House of Representatives shall chuse their Speaker and other Officers; and shall have the sole Power of Impeachment.

Section 3.

The Senate of the United States shall be composed of two Senators from each State, chosen by the Legislature thereof, for six Years; and each Senator shall have one Vote.

Immediately after they shall be assembled in Consequence of the first Election, they shall be divided as equally as may be into three Classes. The Seats of the Senators of the first Class shall be vacated at the Expiration of the second Year, of the second Class at the Expiration of the fourth Year, and of the third Class at the Expiration of the sixth Year, so that one third may be chosen every second Year; and if Vacancies happen by Resignation, or otherwise, during the Recess of the Legislature of any State, the Executive thereof may make temporary Appointments until the next Meeting of the Legislature, which shall then fill such Vacancies.

No Person shall be a Senator who shall not have attained to the Age of thirty Years, and been nine Years a Citizen of the United States, and who shall not, when elected, be an Inhabitant of that State for which he shall be chosen.

The Vice President of the United States shall be President of the Senate, but shall have no Vote, unless they be equally divided.

The Senate shall chuse their other Officers, and also a President pro tempore, in the Absence of the Vice President, or when he shall exercise the Office of President of the United States.

The Senate shall have the sole Power to try all Impeachments. When sitting for that Purpose, they shall be on Oath or Affirmation. When the President of the United States is tried, the Chief Justice shall preside: And no Person shall be convicted without the Concurrence of two thirds of the Members present.

Judgment in Cases of Impeachment shall not extend further than to removal from Office, and disqualification to hold and enjoy any

Office of honor, Trust or Profit under the United States: but the Party convicted shall nevertheless be liable and subject to Indictment, Trial, Judgment and Punishment, according to Law.

Section 4.

The Times, Places and Manner of holding Elections for Senators and Representatives, shall be prescribed in each State by the Legislature thereof; but the Congress may at any time by Law make or alter such Regulations, except as to the Places of chusing Senators.

The Congress shall assemble at least once in every Year, and such Meeting shall be on the first Monday in December, unless they shall by Law appoint a different Day.

Section 5.

Each House shall be the Judge of the Elections, Returns and Qualifications of its own Members, and a Majority of each shall constitute a Quorum to do Business; but a smaller Number may adjourn from day to day, and may be authorized to compel the Attendance of absent Members, in such Manner, and under such Penalties as each House may provide.

Each House may determine the Rules of its Proceedings, punish its Members for disorderly Behaviour, and, with the Concurrence of two thirds, expel a Member.

Each House shall keep a Journal of its Proceedings, and from time to time publish the same, excepting such Parts as may in their Judgment require Secrecy; and the Yeas and Nays of the Members of either House on any question shall, at the Desire of one fifth of those Present, be entered on the Journal.

Neither House, during the Session of Congress, shall, without the Consent of the other, adjourn for more than three days, nor to any other Place than that in which the two Houses shall be sitting.

Section 6.

The Senators and Representatives shall receive a Compensation for their Services, to be ascertained by Law, and paid out of the Treasury of the United States. They shall in all Cases, except Treason, Felony and Breach of the Peace, be privileged from Arrest during their Attendance at the Session of their respective Houses, and in going to and returning from the same; and for any Speech or Debate in either House, they shall not be questioned in any other Place.

No Senator or Representative shall, during the Time for which he was elected, be appointed to any civil Office under the Authority of the United States, which shall have been created, or the Emoluments whereof shall have been encreased during such time; and no Person holding any Office under the United States, shall be a Member of either House during his Continuance in Office.

Section 7.

All Bills for raising Revenue shall originate in the House of Representatives; but the Senate may propose or concur with Amendments as on other Bills.

Every Bill which shall have passed the House of Representatives and the Senate, shall, before it become a Law, be presented to the President of the United States If he approve; he shall sign it, but if not he shall return it, with his Objections to that House in which it shall have originated, who shall enter the Objections at large on their Journal, and proceed to reconsider it. If after such Reconsideration two thirds of that House shall agree to pass the Bill, it shall be sent, together with the Objections, to the other House, by which it shall likewise be reconsidered, and if approved by two thirds of that House, it shall become a Law. But in all such Cases the Votes of both Houses shall be determined by yeas and Nays, and the Names of the Persons voting for and against the Bill shall be entered on the Journal of each House respectively. If any Bill shall not be returned by the President within ten Days (Sundays excepted) after it shall have been presented to him, the Same shall be a Law, in like Manner as if he had signed it, unless the Congress by their Adjournment prevent its Return, in which Case it shall not be a Law.

Every Order, Resolution, or Vote to which the Concurrence of the Senate and House of Representatives may be necessary (except on a question of Adjournment) shall be presented to the President of the United States; and before the Same shall take Effect, shall be approved by him, or being disapproved by him, shall be repassed by two thirds of the Senate and House of Representatives, according to the Rules and Limitations prescribed in the Case of a Bill.

Section 8.

The Congress shall have Power To lay and collect Taxes, Duties, Imposts and Excises, to pay the Debts and provide for the common Defence and general Welfare of the United States; but all

Duties, Imposts and Excises shall be uniform throughout the United States;

To borrow Money on the credit of the United States;

To regulate Commerce with foreign Nations, and among the several States, and with the Indian Tribes;

To establish an uniform Rule of Naturalization, and uniform Laws on the subject of Bankruptcies throughout the United States;

To coin Money, regulate the Value thereof, and of foreign Coin, and fix the Standard of Weights and Measures;

To provide for the Punishment of counterfeiting the Securities and current Coin of the United States;

To establish Post Offices and post Roads;

To promote the Progress of Science and useful Arts, by securing for limited Times to Authors and Inventors the exclusive Right to their respective Writings and Discoveries;

To constitute Tribunals inferior to the supreme Court;

To define and punish Piracies and Felonies committed on the high Seas, and Offences against the Law of Nations;

To declare War, grant Letters of Marque and Reprisal, and make Rules concerning Captures on Land and Water;

To raise and support Armies, but no Appropriation of Money to that Use shall be for a longer Term than two Years;

To provide and maintain a Navy;

To make Rules for the Government and Regulation of the land and naval Forces;

To provide for calling forth the Militia to execute the Laws of the Union, suppress Insurrections and repel Invasions;

To provide for organizing, arming, and disciplining, the Militia, and for governing such Part of them as may be employed in the Service of the United States, reserving to the States respectively, the Appointment of the Officers, and the Authority of training the Militia according to the discipline prescribed by Congress;

To exercise exclusive Legislation in all Cases whatsoever, over such District (not exceeding ten Miles square) as may, by Cession of particular States, and the Acceptance of Congress, become the Seat of the Government of the United States, and to exercise like Authority over all Places purchased by the Consent of the Legislature of the State in which the Same shall be, for the Erection of Forts, Magazines, Arsenals, dock-Yards, and other needful Buildings;—And

To make all Laws which shall be necessary and proper for carrying into Execution the foregoing Powers, and all other Powers vested by this Constitution in the Government of the United States, or in any Department or Officer thereof.

Section 9.

The Migration or Importation of such Persons as any of the States now existing shall think proper to admit, shall not be prohibited by the Congress prior to the Year one thousand eight hundred and eight, but a Tax or duty may be imposed on such Importation, not exceeding ten dollars for each Person.

The Privilege of the Writ of Habeas Corpus shall not be suspended, unless when in Cases of Rebellion or Invasion the public Safety may require it.

No Bill of Attainder or ex post facto Law shall be passed.

No Capitation, or other direct, Tax shall be laid, unless in Proportion to the Census or enumeration herein before directed to be taken.

No Tax or Duty shall be laid on Articles exported from any State.

No Preference shall be given by any Regulation of Commerce or Revenue to the Ports of one State over those of another: nor shall Vessels bound to, or from, one State, be obliged to enter, clear, or pay Duties in another.

No Money shall be drawn from the Treasury, but in Consequence of Appropriations made by Law; and a regular Statement and Account of the Receipts and Expenditures of all public Money shall be published from time to time.

No Title of Nobility shall be granted by the United States: And no Person holding any Office of Profit or Trust under them, shall, without the Consent of the Congress, accept of any present, Emolument, Office, or Title, of any kind whatever, from any King, Prince, or foreign State.

Section 10.

No State shall enter into any Treaty, Alliance, or Confederation; grant Letters of Marque and Reprisal; coin Money; emit Bills of Credit; make any Thing but gold and silver Coin a Tender in Payment of Debts; pass any Bill of Attainder, ex post facto Law, or Law impairing the Obligation of Contracts, or grant any Title of Nobility.

No State shall, without the Consent of the Congress, lay any Imposts or Duties on Imports or Exports, except what may be absolutely necessary for executing it's inspection Laws: and the net Produce of all Duties and Imposts, laid by any State on Imports or Exports, shall be for the Use of the Treasury of the United States; and all such Laws shall be subject to the Revision and Controul of the Congress.

No State shall, without the Consent of Congress, lay any Duty of Tonnage, keep Troops, or Ships of War in time of Peace, enter into any Agreement or Compact with another State, or with a foreign Power, or engage in War, unless actually invaded, or in such imminent Danger as will not admit of delay.

Article II.

Section 1.

The executive Power shall be vested in a President of the United States of America. He shall hold his Office during the Term of four Years, and, together with the Vice President, chosen for the same Term, be elected, as follows

Each State shall appoint, in such Manner as the Legislature thereof may direct, a Number of Electors, equal to the whole Number of Senators and Representatives to which the State may be entitled in the Congress: but no Senator or Representative, or Person holding an Office of Trust or Profit under the United States, shall be appointed an Elector.

The Electors shall meet in their respective States, and vote by Ballot for two Persons, of whom one at least shall not be an Inhabitant of the same State with themselves. And they shall make a List of all the Persons voted for, and of the Number of Votes for each; which List they shall sign and certify, and transmit sealed to the Seat of the Government of the United States, directed to the President of the Senate. The President of the Senate shall, in the Presence of the Senate and House of Representatives, open all the Certificates, and the Votes shall then be counted. The Person having the greatest Number of Votes shall be the President, if such Number be a Majority of the whole Number of Electors appointed; and if there be more than one who have such Majority, and have an equal Number of Votes, then the House of Representatives shall immediately chuse by Ballot one of them for President; and if no Person have a Majority, then from the five highest on the List the said House shall in like Manner chuse the President. But in chusing the President, the Votes shall be taken by States, the Representation from each State having one Vote; A quorum for this Purpose shall consist of a Member or Members from two thirds of the States, and a Majority of all the States shall be necessary to a Choice. In every Case, after the Choice of the President, the Person having the greatest Number of Votes of the Electors shall be the Vice President. But if there should remain two or more who have equal Votes, the Senate shall chuse from them by Ballot the Vice President.

The Congress may determine the Time of chusing the Electors, and the Day on which they shall give their Votes; which Day shall be the same throughout the United States.

No Person except a natural born Citizen, or a Citizen of the United States, at the time of the Adoption of this Constitution, shall be eligible to the Office of President; neither shall any Person be eligible to that Office who shall not have attained to the Age of thirty five Years, and been fourteen Years a Resident within the United States.

In Case of the Removal of the President from Office, or of his Death, Resignation, or Inability to discharge the Powers and Duties of the said Office, the Same shall devolve on the Vice President, and the Congress may by Law provide for the Case of Removal, Death, Resignation or Inability, both of the President and Vice President, declaring what Officer shall then act as President, and such Officer shall act accordingly, until the Disability be removed, or a President shall be elected.

The President shall, at stated Times, receive for his Services, a Compensation, which shall neither be encreased nor diminished during the Period for which he shall have been elected, and he shall not receive within that Period any other Emolument from the United States, or any of them.

Before he enter on the Execution of his Office, he shall take the following Oath or Affirmation:—"I do solemnly swear (or affirm) that I will faithfully execute the Office of President of the United States, and will to the best of my Ability, preserve, protect and defend the Constitution of the United States."

Section 2.

The President shall be Commander in Chief of the Army and Navy of the United States, and of the Militia of the several States, when called into the actual Service of the United States; he may require the Opinion, in writing, of the principal Officer in each of the executive

Departments, upon any Subject relating to the Duties of their respective Offices, and he shall have Power to grant Reprieves and Pardons for Offences against the United States, except in Cases of Impeachment.

He shall have Power, by and with the Advice and Consent of the Senate, to make Treaties, provided two thirds of the Senators present concur; and he shall nominate, and by and with the Advice and Consent of the Senate, shall appoint Ambassadors, other public Ministers and Consuls, Judges of the supreme Court, and all other Officers of the United States, whose Appointments are not herein otherwise provided for, and which shall be established by Law: but the Congress may by Law vest the Appointment of such inferior Officers, as they think proper, in the President alone, in the Courts of Law, or in the Heads of Departments.

The President shall have Power to fill up all Vacancies that may happen during the Recess of the Senate, by granting Commissions which shall expire at the End of their next Session.

Section 3.

He shall from time to time give to the Congress Information of the State of the Union, and recommend to their Consideration such Measures as he shall judge necessary and expedient; he may, on extraordinary Occasions, convene both Houses, or either of them, and in Case of Disagreement between them, with Respect to the Time of Adjournment, he may adjourn them to such Time as he shall think proper; he shall receive Ambassadors and other public Ministers; he shall take Care that the Laws be faithfully executed, and shall Commission all the Officers of the United States.

Section 4.

The President, Vice President and all civil Officers of the United States, shall be removed from Office on Impeachment for, and Conviction of, Treason, Bribery, or other high Crimes and Misdemeanors.

Article III.

Section 1.

The judicial Power of the United States, shall be vested in one supreme Court, and in such inferior Courts as the Congress may from time to time ordain and establish. The Judges, both of the supreme and inferior Courts, shall hold their Offices during good Behaviour, and shall, at stated Times, receive for their Services, a Compensation, which shall not be diminished during their Continuance in Office.

Section 2.

The judicial Power shall extend to all Cases, in Law and Equity, arising under this Constitution, the Laws of the United States, and Treaties made, or which shall be made, under their Authority;—to all Cases affecting Ambassadors, other public Ministers and Consuls;—to all Cases of admiralty and maritime Jurisdiction;—to Controversies to which the United States shall be a Party;—to Controversies between two or more States;— between a State and Citizens of another State,—between Citizens of different States,—between Citizens of the same State claiming Lands under Grants of different States, and between a State, or the Citizens thereof, and foreign States, Citizens or Subjects.

In all Cases affecting Ambassadors, other public Ministers and Consuls, and those in which a State shall be Party, the supreme Court shall have original Jurisdiction. In all the other Cases before mentioned, the supreme Court shall have appellate Jurisdiction, both as to Law and Fact, with such Exceptions, and under such Regulations as the Congress shall make.

The Trial of all Crimes, except in Cases of Impeachment, shall be by Jury; and such Trial shall be held in the State where the said Crimes shall have been committed; but when not committed within any State, the Trial shall be at such Place or Places as the Congress may by Law have directed.

Section 3.

Treason against the United States, shall consist only in levying War against them, or in adhering to their Enemies, giving them Aid and Comfort. No Person shall be convicted of Treason unless on the Testimony of two Witnesses to the same overt Act, or on Confession in open Court.

The Congress shall have Power to declare the Punishment of Treason, but no Attainder of Treason shall work Corruption of Blood, or Forfeiture except during the Life of the Person attainted.

Article IV.

Section 1.

Full Faith and Credit shall be given in each State to the public Acts, Records, and judicial Proceedings of every other State. And the Congress may by general Laws prescribe the Manner in which such Acts, Records and Proceedings shall be proved, and the Effect thereof.

Section 2.

The Citizens of each State shall be entitled to all Privileges and Immunities of Citizens in the several States.

A Person charged in any State with Treason, Felony, or other Crime, who shall flee from Justice, and be found in another State, shall on Demand of the executive Authority of the State from which he fled, be delivered up, to be removed to the State having Jurisdiction of the Crime.

No Person held to Service or Labour in one State, under the Laws thereof, escaping into another, shall, in Consequence of any Law or Regulation therein, be discharged from such Service or Labour, but shall be delivered up on Claim of the Party to whom such Service or Labour may be due.

Section 3.

New States may be admitted by the Congress into this Union; but no new State shall be formed or erected within the Jurisdiction of any other State; nor any State be formed by the Junction of two or more States, or Parts of States, without the Consent of the Legislatures of the States concerned as well as of the Congress.

The Congress shall have Power to dispose of and make all needful Rules and Regulations respecting the Territory or other Property belonging to the United States; and nothing in this Constitution shall be so construed as to Prejudice any Claims of the United States, or of any particular State.

Section 4.

The United States shall guarantee to every State in this Union a Republican Form of Government, and shall protect each of them against Invasion; and on Application of the Legislature, or of the Executive (when the Legislature cannot be convened), against domestic Violence.

Article V.

The Congress, whenever two thirds of both Houses shall deem it necessary, shall propose Amendments to this Constitution, or, on the Application of the Legislatures of two thirds of the several States, shall call a Convention for proposing Amendments, which, in either Case, shall be valid to all Intents and Purposes, as Part of this Constitution, when ratified by the Legislatures of three fourths of the several States, or by Conventions in three fourths thereof, as the one or the other Mode of Ratification may be proposed by the Congress; Provided that no Amendment which may be made prior to the Year One thousand eight hundred and eight shall in any Manner affect the first and fourth Clauses in the Ninth Section of the first Article; and that no State, without its Consent, shall be deprived of its equal Suffrage in the Senate.

Article VI.

All Debts contracted and Engagements entered into, before the Adoption of this Constitution, shall be as valid against the United States under this Constitution, as under the Confederation.

This Constitution, and the Laws of the United States which shall be made in Pursuance thereof; and all Treaties made, or which shall be made, under the Authority of the United States, shall be the supreme Law of the Land; and the Judges in every State shall be bound thereby, any Thing in the Constitution or Laws of any State to the Contrary notwithstanding.

The Senators and Representatives before mentioned, and the Members of the several State Legislatures, and all executive and judicial Officers, both of the United States and of the several States, shall be bound by Oath or Affirmation, to support this Constitution; but no religious Test shall ever be required as a Qualification to any Office or public Trust under the United States.

Article VII.

The Ratification of the Conventions of nine States, shall be sufficient for the Establishment of this Constitution between the States so ratifying the Same.

The Word, "the," being interlined between the seventh and eighth Lines of the first Page, The Word "Thirty" being partly written on an Erazure in the fifteenth Line of the first Page, The Words "is tried" being interlined between the thirty second and thirty third Lines of the first Page and the Word "the" being interlined between the forty third and forty fourth Lines of the second Page.

Attest William Jackson Secretary

done in Convention by the Unanimous Consent of the States present the Seventeenth Day of September in the Year of our Lord one thousand seven hundred and Eighty seven and of the Independence of the United States of America the Twelfth In witness whereof We have hereunto subscribed our Names...

Amendments I through X
The Bill of Rights

Amendment I

Congress shall make no law respecting an establishment of religion, or prohibiting the free exercise thereof; or abridging the freedom of speech, or of the press; or the right of the people peaceably to assemble, and to petition the Government for a redress of grievances.

Amendment II

A well regulated Militia, being necessary to the security of a free State, the right of the people to keep and bear Arms shall not be infringed.

Amendment III

No Soldier shall, in time of peace be quartered in any house, without the consent of the Owner, nor in time of war, but in a manner to be prescribed by law.

Amendment IV

The right of the people to be secure in their persons, houses, papers, and effects, against unreasonable searches and seizures shall not be violated, and no Warrants shall issue , but upon probable cause, supported by Oath or affirmation, and particularly describing the place to be searched, and the persons or things to be seized.

Amendment V

No person shall be held to answer for a capital, or otherwise infamous crime, unless on a presentment or indictment of a Grand Jury, except in cases arising in the land or naval forces, or in the Militia, when in actual service in time of War or public danger; nor shall any person be subject for the same offence to be twice put in jeopardy of life or limb; nor shall be compelled in any criminal case to be a witness against himself, nor be deprived of life, liberty, or property, without due process of law; nor shall private property be taken for public use, without just compensation.

Amendment VI

In all criminal prosecutions, the accused shall enjoy the right to a speedy and public trial, by an impartial jury of the State and district wherein the crime shall have been committed, which district shall have been previously ascertained by law, and to be informed of the nature and cause of the accusation; to be confronted with the witnesses against him; to have compulsory process for obtaining witnesses in his favor, and to have the Assistance of Counsel for his defence.

Amendment VII

In Suits at common law, where the value in controversy shall exceed twenty dollars, the right of trial by jury shall be preserved, and no fact tried by a jury, shall be otherwise re-examined in any Court of the United States, than according to the rules of the common law.

Amendment VIII

Excessive bail shall not be required, nor excessive fines imposed, nor cruel and unusual punishments inflicted.

Amendment IX

The enumeration in the Constitution, of certain rights, shall not be construed to deny or disparage others retained by the people.

Amendment X

The powers not delegated to the United States by the Constitution, nor prohibited by it to the States, are reserved to the States respectively, or to the people.

Amendments XI through XXVII

Amendment XI

The Judicial power of the United States shall not be construed to extend to any suit in law or equity, commenced or prosecuted against one of the United States by Citizens of another State, or by Citizens or Subjects of any Foreign State.

Amendment XII

The Electors shall meet in their respective states and vote by ballot for President and Vice-President, one of whom, at least, shall not be an inhabitant of the same state with themselves; they shall name in their ballots the person voted for as President, and in distinct ballots the person voted for as Vice-President, and they shall make distinct lists of all persons voted for as President, and of all persons voted for as Vice-President, and of the number of votes for each, which lists they shall sign and certify, and transmit sealed to the seat of the government of the United States, directed to the President of the Senate.

The President of the Senate shall, in the presence of the Senate and House of Representatives, open all the certificates and the votes shall then be counted.

The person having the greatest number of votes for President, shall be the President, if such number be a majority of the whole number of Electors appointed; and if no person have such majority, then from the persons having the highest numbers not exceeding three on the list of those voted for as President, the House of Representatives shall choose immediately, by ballot, the President. But in choosing the President, the votes shall be taken by states, the representation from each state having one vote; a quorum for this purpose shall consist of a member or members from two-thirds of the states, and a majority of all the states shall be necessary to a choice. And if the House of Representatives shall not choose a President whenever the right of choice shall devolve upon them, before the fourth day of March next following, then the Vice-President shall act as President, as in case of the death or other constitutional disability of the President.

The person having the greatest number of votes as Vice-President, shall be the Vice-President, if such number be a majority of the whole number of Electors appointed, and if no person have a majority, then from the two highest numbers on the list, the Senate shall choose the Vice-President; a quorum for the purpose shall consist of two-thirds of the whole number of Senators, and a majority of the whole number shall be necessary to a choice. But no person constitutionally ineligible to the office of President shall be eligible to that of Vice-President of the United States.

Amendment XIII
Section 1.

Neither slavery nor involuntary servitude, except as a punishment for crime whereof the party shall have been duly convicted, shall exist within the United States , or any place subject to their jurisdiction.

Section 2.

Congress shall have power to enforce this article by appropriate legislation.

Amendment XIV

Section 1.

All persons born or naturalized in the United States, and subject to the jurisdiction thereof, are citizens of the United States and of the State wherein they reside. No State shall make or enforce any law which shall abridge the privileges or immunities of citizens of the United States; nor shall any State deprive any person of life, liberty, or property, without due process of law; nor deny to any person within its jurisdiction the equal protection of the laws.

Section 2.

Representatives shall be apportioned among the several States according to their respective numbers, counting the whole number of persons in each State, excluding Indians not taxed. But when the right to vote at any election for the choice of electors for President and Vice-President of the United States, Representatives in Congress, the Executive and Judicial officers of a State, or the members of the Legislature thereof, is denied to any of the male inhabitants of such State, being twenty-one years of age, and citizens of the United States, or in any way abridged, except for participation in rebellion, or other crime, the basis of representation therein shall be reduced in the proportion which the number of such male citizens shall bear to the whole number of male citizens twenty-one years of age in such State.

Section 3.

No person shall be a Senator or Representative in Congress, or elector of President and Vice-President, or hold any office, civil or military, under the United States, or under any State, who, having previously taken an oath, as a member of Congress, or as an officer of the United States, or as a member of any State legislature, or as an executive or judicial officer of any State, to support the Constitution of the United States, shall have engaged in insurrection or rebellion against the same, or given aid or comfort to the enemies thereof. But Congress may by a vote of two-thirds of each House, remove such disability.

Section 4.

The validity of the public debt of the United States, authorized by law, including debts incurred for payment of pensions and bounties for services in suppressing insurrection or rebellion, shall not be questioned. But neither the United States nor any State shall assume or pay any debt or obligation incurred in aid of insurrection or rebellion against the United States, or any claim for the loss or emancipation of any slave; but all such debts, obligations and claims shall be held illegal and void.

Section 5.

The Congress shall have the power to enforce, by appropriate legislation, the provisions of this article.

Amendment XV
Section 1.

The right of citizens of the United States to vote shall not be denied or abridged by the United States or by any State on account of race, color, or previous condition of servitude

Section 2.

The Congress shall have the power to enforce this article by appropriate legislation.

Amendment XVI

The Congress shall have power to lay and collect taxes on incomes, from whatever source derived, without apportionment among the several States, and without regard to any census or enumeration.

Amendment XVII

The Senate of the United States shall be composed of two Senators from each State, elected by the people thereof, for six years; and each Senator shall have one vote. the electors in each State shall have the qualifications requisite for electors of the most numerous branch of the State legislatures.

When vacancies happen in the representation of any State in the Senate, the executive authority of such State shall issue writs of election to fill such vacancies: Provided, that the legislature of any State may empower the executive thereof to make temporary appointments until the people fill the vacancies by election as the legislature may direct.

This amendment shall not be so construed as to affect the election or term of any Senator chosen before it becomes valid as part of the Constitution.

Amendment XVIII

Section 1.

After one year from the ratification of this article the manufacture, sale, or transportation of intoxicating liquors within, the importation thereof into, or the exportation thereof from the United States and all territory subject to the jurisdiction thereof for beverage purposes is hereby prohibited.

Section 2.

The Congress and the several States shall have concurrent power to enforce this article by appropriate legislation.

Section 3.

This article shall be inoperative unless it shall have been ratified as an amendment to the Constitution by the legislatures of the several States, as provided in the Constitution, within seven years from the date of the submission hereof to the States by the Congress.

Amendment XIX

The right of citizens of the United States to vote shall not be denied or abridged by the United States or by any State on account of sex.

Congress shall have power to enforce this article by appropriate legislation.

Amendment XX

Section 1.

The terms of the President and the Vice President shall end at noon on the 20th day of January, and the terms of Senators and Representatives at noon on the 3d day of January, of the years in which such terms would have ended if this article had not been ratified; and the terms of their successors shall then begin.

Section 2.

The Congress shall assemble at least once in every year, and such meeting shall begin at noon on the 3d day of January, unless they shall by law appoint a different day.

Section 3.

If, at the time fixed for the beginning of the term of the President, the President elect shall have died, the Vice President elect shall become President. If a President shall not have been chosen before the time fixed for the beginning of his term, or if the President elect shall have failed to qualify, then the Vice President elect shall act as President until a President shall have qualified; and the Congress may by law provide for the case wherein neither a President elect nor a Vice President shall have qualified, declaring who shall then act as President, or the manner in which one who is to act shall be selected, and such person shall act accordingly until a President or Vice President shall have qualified.

Section 4.

The Congress may by law provide for the case of the death of any of the persons from whom the House of Representatives may choose a President whenever the right of choice shall have devolved upon them, and for the case of the death of any of the persons from whom the Senate may choose a Vice President whenever the right of choice shall have devolved upon them.

Section 5.

Sections 1 and 2 shall take effect on the 15th day of October following the ratification of this article.

Section 6.

This article shall be inoperative unless it shall have been ratified as an amendment to the Constitution by the legislatures of three-fourths of the several States within seven years from the date of its submission.

Amendment XXI

Section 1.

The eighteenth article of amendment to the Constitution of the United States is hereby repealed.

Section 2.

The transportation or importation into any State, territory, or Possession of the United States for delivery or use therein of intoxicating liquors, in violation of the laws thereof, is hereby prohibited.

Section 3.

This article shall be inoperative unless it shall have been ratified as an amendment to the Constitution by conventions in the several States, as provided in the Constitution, within seven years from the date of the submission hereof to the States by the Congress.

Amendment XXII
Section 1.

No person shall be elected to the office of the President more than twice, and no person who has held the office of President, or acted as President, for more than two years of a term to which some other person was elected President shall be elected to the office of President more than once~~51~~. But this Article shall not apply to any person holding the office of President when this Article was proposed by Congress, and shall not prevent any person who may be holding the office of President, or acting as President, during the term within which this Article becomes operative from holding the office of President or acting as President during the remainder of such term.
Section 2.

This article shall be inoperative unless it shall have been ratified as an amendment to the Constitution by the legislatures of three-fourths of the several States within seven years from the date of its submission to the States by the Congress.

Amendment XXIII
Section 1.

The District constituting the seat of Government of the United States shall appoint in such manner as Congress may direct:

A number of electors of President and Vice President equal to the whole number of Senators and Representatives in Congress to which the District would be entitled if it were a State, but in no event more than the least populous State; they shall be in addition to those appointed by the States, but they shall be considered, for the purposes of the election of President and Vice President, to be electors appointed by a State; and they shall meet in the District and perform such duties as provided by the twelfth article of amendment.
Section 2.

The Congress shall have power to enforce this article by appropriate legislation.

Amendment XXIV
Section 1.

The right of citizens of the United States to vote in any primary or other election for President or Vice President, for electors for President or Vice President, or for Senator or Representative in Congress, shall not be denied or abridged by the United States or any State by reason of failure to pay poll tax or other tax.

Section 2.

The Congress shall have power to enforce this article by appropriate legislation.

Amendment XXV
Section 1.

In case of the removal of the President from office or of his death or resignation, the Vice President shall become President.

Section 2.

Whenever there is a vacancy in the office of the Vice President, the President shall nominate a Vice President who shall take office upon confirmation by a majority vote of both Houses of Congress.

Section 3.

Whenever the President transmits to the President pro tempore of the Senate and the Speaker of the House of Representatives his written declaration that he is unable to discharge the powers and duties of his office, and until he transmits to them a written declaration to the contrary, such powers and duties shall be discharged by the Vice President as Acting President.

Section 4.

Whenever the Vice President and a majority of either the principal officers of the executive departments or of such other body as Congress may by law provide, transmit to the President pro tempore of the Senate and the Speaker of the House of Representatives their written declaration that the President is unable to discharge the powers and duties of his office, the Vice President shall immediately assume the powers and duties of the office as Acting President.

Thereafter, when the President transmits to the President pro tempore of the Senate and the Speaker of the House of Representatives his written declaration that no inability exists, he shall resume the powers and duties of his office unless the Vice President and a majority of either the principal officers of the executive department or of such other body as Congress may by law provide, transmit within four days to the President pro tempore of the Senate and the Speaker of the House of Representatives their written declaration that the President is unable to discharge the powers and duties of his office. Thereupon Congress shall decide the issue, assembling within forty-eight hours for that purpose if not in session. If the Congress, within twenty-one days after receipt of the latter written declaration, or, if Congress is not in session, within twenty-one days after Congress is required to assemble, determines by two-thirds vote of both Houses that the President is unable to discharge the powers and duties of his office, the Vice President shall continue to discharge the same as Acting President; otherwise, the President shall resume the powers and duties of his office.

Amendment XXVI

Section 1.

The right of citizens of the United States, who are eighteen years of age or older, to vote shall not be denied or abridged by the United States or by any State on account of age.

Section 2.

The Congress shall have power to enforce this article by appropriate legislation.

Amendment XXVII

No law, varying the compensation for the services of the Senators and Representatives, shall take effect, until an election of representatives shall have intervened.